1980

W9-CMN-480

CHINA REVISITED
After Forty-two Years

by the same author

THE CHINESE EYE
CHINESE PAINTING
CHINESE CALLIGRAPHY
A CHINESE CHILDHOOD

BIRDS AND BEASTS
CHINPAO AND THE GIANT PANDAS
CHINPAO AT THE ZOO
LO CHENG, THE BOY WHO WOULDN'T KEEP STILL
THE MEN OF THE BURMA ROAD
A STORY OF MING
DABBITSE
YEBBIN

THE SILENT TRAVELLER IN LAKELAND
THE SILENT TRAVELLER IN LONDON
THE SILENT TRAVELLER IN WARTIME
THE SILENT TRAVELLER IN THE YORKSHIRE DALES
THE SILENT TRAVELLER IN OXFORD
THE SILENT TRAVELLER IN EDINBURGH
THE SILENT TRAVELLER IN NEW YORK
THE SILENT TRAVELLER IN DUBLIN
THE SILENT TRAVELLER IN PARIS
THE SILENT TRAVELLER IN BOSTON
THE SILENT TRAVELLER IN SAN FRANCISCO
THE SILENT TRAVELLER IN JAPAN

''The river and mountain are so beautiful like this!'' A line from one of Mao Tse-tung's poems.

CHINA REVISITED

After Forty-two Years

written and illustrated
by
CHIANG YEE
''The Silent Traveller''

W · W · NORTON & COMPANY · INC · NEW YORK

COPYRIGHT © 1977 BY W. W. NORTON & COMPANY, INC.
ALL RIGHTS RESERVED
Published simultaneously in Canada
by George J. McLeod Limited, Toronto

First Edition

Library of Congress Cataloging in Publication Data

Chiang, Yee, 1903–
  China revisited, after forty-two years.

  1. China—Description and travel—1949–
2. Chiang, Yee, 1903– I. Title.
DS711.C4643 1977   951.04'092'4 [B]   77-22587
ISBN 0-393-08791-3

1 2 3 4 5 6 7 8 9 0

Contents

Chinese Dynasties

Shang	ca. 1523–1028 B.C.
Middle Shang	15–13 century B.C.
Late Shang	15–11 century B.C.
Chou	ca. 1027–222 B.C.
Western Chou	ca. 1027–771 B.C.
Early	ca. 1027–948 B.C.
Middle	ca. 948–858 B.C.
Late	ca. 858–771 B.C.
Ch'un'Ch'iu	770–481 B.C.
Warring States	480–222 B.C.
Ch'in	221–207 B.C.
Han	206 B.C.–A.D. 220
Western Han	206 B.C.–A.D. 8
Wang Mang Interregnum	A.D. 9–24
Eastern Han	A.D. 25–220
The Three Kingdoms	A.D. 220–265
Western Chin	A.D. 265–313
Eastern Chin	A.D. 317–419
Wei	A.D. 385–557
Northern Ch'i	A.D. 550–577
Northern Chou	A.D. 557–580
Sui	A.D. 581–618
T'ang	A.D. 618–908
Five Dynasties	A.D. 907–960
Northern Sung	A.D. 960–1127
Southern Sung	A.D. 1127–1279
Yüan	A.D. 1279–1368
Ming	A.D. 1368–1644
Ch'ing	A.D. 1644–1912

CHINA REVISITED
After Forty-two Years

Prologue

I WAS FORCED to leave my homeland in 1933. I did not plan to stay abroad for more than a year or so, partly for lack of funds and partly because my heart was torn by reports of disasters involving many of my kinsmen. However, in July 1937 the Japanese Army invaded China and this proved to be the beginning of a full-scale Sino-Japanese war. After the bombing of Pearl Harbor by Japan, America immediately joined the great struggle against Nazism and Fascism and China became a partner of the Allies in World War II. Though I had been anxious to return home since 1937, it was not possible then to get a passage.

World War II ended in 1945, but war did not end in China, for civil strife flared up again and intensified throughout the country. It was even more difficult for me to go back to my homeland, and I was recommended for a teaching position in New York. That was about the time of McCarthyism and the movement to crush "un-American" activities was probing into every part of American life. It was impossible even to express in public my wish to see my homeland again. However, the tide turned in the early 1970s. President Richard Nixon was received in Peking and the representative of the People's Republic of China took his rightful seat at the United Nations. The relationship between America and China became easier: more news of China appeared in the daily papers of a very different nature from the reports of conditions in the years before 1949. From 1933 to 1949 China had been a country terribly torn, in which the majority of the general populace had not a moment of peace; a large portion of them had little to eat and many died of starvation.

Who would not want to take this opportunity to see China, particularly a Chinese like me who had left four young children at home when he rushed abroad? Many were making the trip when I retired from Columbia University in 1971. But I could not immediately follow their example, for I had committed myself to teach in Hong Kong for six months and then in Australia for the year 1972–73.

I had been absent from China for forty-two years, nearly half a century. Half a century is a long time. During those forty-two years I had seen many changes taking place in England and America. The changes that had taken place in China since 1933 could have been even greater. I was so anxious and curious to learn about these great changes that I read whatever accounts I could get hold of in the daily papers and also in books written by people who had recently made visits to China. But a Chinese popular saying, "Seeing once is better than hearing about it a hundred times," kept telling me that I must go to see the changes myself. At last an opportunity came. I flew to Canton via Hong Kong on April 15, 1975, and managed to stay in China for two months. My two daughters and their husbands traveled about with me to a number of places, and during those sixty days I made notes of my personal impressions, of everything I saw and discussed with my children. These form the basis of the present book, which is an account of my personal experiences in China before 1933 and forty-two years later.

The contrast between these two periods of China's history is clear to see. I have not indulged in exaggeration or described anything I have not actually seen. In places I may have unavoidably given a generalized view of things, for there was no room to go into detail. Though the changes I saw and experienced may have been recorded differently in the writings of others, I must remind my readers that I am a China-born Chinese who lived in China for thirty years and who has two daughters and their husbands (all high school teachers), together with their seven children, to give me a deeper insight and interpretation. I have set down everything as faithfully as I could according to my own judgment. My records end on June 15, 1975. But I am confident that any future changes will be for the better not for the worse as far as China is concerned. China, formerly known as a backward country, at present is a brand-new nation, only twenty-six years in the making, with masses of things to be done by her eight hundred million people working together with a united spirit.

I

Why I Left China for England

EVER SINCE China was defeated in the Opium War with England, in many subsequent wars with other Western powers, and in the Sino-Japanese War of 1894, most Chinese realized that their country had a lot to learn from abroad. But the jealous Manchu rulers dreaded any influx of foreign ideas which might weaken their grip, so they hesitated to encourage the young generation to study in the West or in Japan. Then China was severely defeated again in the Boxer Uprising in 1900 by the forces of eight Western allies including the United States. Among the terms of the treaty then signed was the payment of a heavy indemnity by the Chinese government to each of the allied forces. In addition to signing many unequal treaties, China had to open a number of treaty ports. The allied countries could exercise extraterritorial rights within their "concessions" in any of these treaty ports. Not only that, certain personnel were selected by agreement of the allied countries to operate the Chinese postal services and customs there. As far as I can remember, those officials were English generally, for they feared that China might not pay the indemnity.

However, America did not accept the indemnity as such, but with the money set up Tsing-hua College in Peking to train young Chinese from about fourteen years old to be sent to America for higher study. From 1912 onward hundreds and thousands of young Chinese students left for colleges and universities in the United States. Those who had studied in America generally had more opportunities for a good position when they returned to China. In addition to these selected from Tsing-hua College, many other youngsters from rich families also went abroad to study. To study abroad then became a fashion, but only the well-to-do could afford it unless a youngster could win a government scholarship. Like many other college graduates I joined the crowd in trying to win a scholarship, but failed the examination chiefly because my knowledge of English was not up to the standard. I mention this in order to explain that I went to England later, at the age of thirty, for a very different reason.

I was born in 1903, a few years after the first Sino-Japanese War of 1894 when China suffered a great defeat and had to hand over to Japan, in addition to many other things, the island of Formosa (i.e., Taiwan). As a youngster I was not allowed to go out by myself till I was over ten years old, but within doors I passed for the most part a perfectly happy life, as I recorded in an earlier book *A Chi-*

nese Childhood. My mother died when I was five and my father died when I was eighteen. I was raised by my grandmother with the help of my elder sister. In my early teens I was well tutored in the family school and learned to read widely. Then I went to middle school (equivalent to high school in America) for three years and read in history textbooks about the Opium War, the Tai-ping Rebellion, the Sino-Japanese War, the Boxer Uprising, and Dr. Sun Yat-sen's anti-Manchu movement. After my sister entered a missionary school, to please the young man to whom she was engaged, our home began to hear about some Christian teachings. Those teachings kept my young head wondering why the God-fearing English and Americans, too, could have pushed the sale of that poisonous opium on us Chinese without any fear of punishment from God. Had they forgotten to "love thy neighbor as thyself"? This may have been the basic reason why I was never converted to Christianity.

My grandmother was a kind, sensible, and fair-minded person who ran the family affairs according to the age-old Chinese tradition. Despite all the troubles China had with foreign powers and the unrest among the masses, there was a tolerant peaceful atmosphere within my home. My grandfather, though passing his whole life under Manchu rule, never supported the Manchus in his heart. He insisted on wearing a style of dress belonging to the former Ming dynasty, whose rulers were of genuine Chinese Han stock. But the Manchus' literary inquisition was very severe and many scholars were sentenced to death merely for having written some words or expression which implied a criticism of the Manchu emperor. No one then dared to express his disagreement with the authorities. My grandfather managed to keep his thoughts to himself all his life.

The first Manchu emperor of China, a strong man with soldiers of his own race well trained in Manchuria, defeated the last weak emperor of the Ming dynasty in 1644, entered China, and set up a new dynasty, the Ching. At that time his Manchurian soldiers, fresh from victory, were seasoned and good fighters. They were all descendants of the royal race and received special treatment above the Chinese and other minorities in China. Later generations of them became well-to-do and soft, and by the beginning of the nineteenth century very few Manchurians were rank-and-file soldiers; instead, a good many rose to be generals and commanders without much experience in warfare. They did not realize their shortcomings and maintained a haughty and arrogant attitude toward foreigners. Just before the outbreak of the Opium War, a memorandum saying, "Without despising the enemy, we have no cause to fear them," was sent to the emperor. The thin eggshell was soon broken by the English bullets and there was no way to keep the white and yolk together. Hence one defeat followed another. After many defeats by the Western powers and Japan, the Manchu emperor and his royal associates decided to set up a college to train leaders for a new army. The first such college was Peiyang Military Academy.

China did not end her troubles when the Manchu rulers were thrown out and she became a republic in 1911. Dr. Sun Yat-sen, the leader of the anti-Manchu revolution and the founder of the Chinese Republic, was selected the first provisional president, but unfortunately he did not build up a sufficiently strong force to back up the newly established government and he had to yield to the most powerful man of the time—Yüan Shih-kai. Yüan Shih-kai was not a Manchu but a Chinese born in Honan Province. He rose to become the governor of Chihli Province but later retired because of some differences with his immediate superior. Yüan Shih-kai had been head of the Peiyang Military Academy. He was summoned from his retirement to represent the Manchus, in negotiating peace with the revolutionary forces led by Dr. Sun Yat-sen. Yüan Shih-kai was very shrewd. He immediately changed sides and was elected president of the Republic of China to succeed Dr. Sun, with the backing of all the former government armies which now had very few Manchu soldiers—they were almost entirely Chinese.

Yüan Shih-kai never understood what a republic meant. Being well acquainted with the imperial court life in his early days, he secretly planned to make himself emperor. He acquired the support of many provincial governors who were former students of the Peiyang Military Academy and had received their training under him or had been befriended by him. He enthroned himself under the reigning title of Hung Hsien. But Dr. Sun Yat-sen's followers in southwest China rose up against him, and he only managed to be so-called emperor for eighty days.

Though Yüan Shih-kai was pulled down and soon died, and China became a republic again, Dr. Sun Yat-sen was not invited to resume his position. General Li Yüan-hung had been elected vice-president under Yüan Shih-kai and he now assumed the post of president with General Tuan Chi-jui as prime minister. Both Li and Tuan belonged to the Peiyang army clique, together with others who were governors of different provinces. Thus the Chinese government, central and provincial, was in the hands of army men from 1914 to 1928. They were known as war lords.

The term *war lord* was then a new one in the Chinese dictionary. Each general held a large number of soldiers whose loyalty was not to the country but to the general himself. If the general was the governor of a province, he could feed his soldiers from the land taxes of the area and the soldiers in turn did for him whatever he fancied, for he had the law in his own hands. Thus he was termed "warlord of the province." War-lordism was a term created to describe their behavior. War-lordism has something in common with feudalism, but the war lords were worse than the feudal princes for they were usually illiterate and notorious for their evil ways. They never considered they ought to do something for the people, but instead tried to squeeze as much out of them as possible. While the Chinese people suffered much from famine, drought, and floods, the war lords added still more to their miseries. Yet each of the war lords kept a number of the so-called Confucian scholars to work for him. But no ordinary Chinese liked even to pronounce their names.

An old peasant trying to uproot a big rock.

Throughout past centuries Chinese soldiers historically have not been conscripted. A popular saying in China is 好鐵不打釘好漢不當兵, or *"Hao tieh
pu ta ting, hao han pu tan ping"* which means "Good iron is not used to make
nails, a good man will not go for a soldier." But why were the war lords never
short of soldiers? It was simply because men were driven to soldiering as an al-
ternative to starvation. Theodore H. White wrote, "Famine and flood are
China's sorrow. From time out of mind Chinese chronicles have recorded these
recurrent disasters with a beating, persistent note of doom." From a study completed by the American Student Agricultural Society, the surprising and significant fact came to light that between the years 108 B.C. and A.D. 1911 there were
1,828 famines in China, or one for nearly every year in one or another province.
Many men joined an army in order to get something to eat and to keep alive. The
old Chinese term for soldiers was 吃餉的, *Chih-hsiang-ti,* or 吃糧的,
Chih-liang-ti, which means "rice soldier"; similarly, the early Chinese converts
to Christianity who underwent conversion in order to get something to eat from
the missionaries were called 吃教的, *Chih-chiao-ti,* or "one who gets food from
religion," "rice Christian." The rice soldiers had no idea about how to go about
the task of defending their country; they just followed anybody who would give
them food. They had no sense of being the national army, so it was little wonder
that China was defeated again and again. It is remarkable that the Manchu rulers
and their ministers never devised a method of conscripting young men and training them to maintain their grip on the country. I have read my family clan book
which dates back to the Western Han dynasty, about the third century B.C. Down
to my generation not one of the sons from the Chiang family had been conscripted as a soldier.

I must go back to the years when Yüan Shih-kai was the second elected
president of the Republic about to enthrone himself as a new emperor. When
World War I broke out, Japan was clever enough to join the side of the Allies in

order to seize the German leasehold in China around Kiaochow Bay and also the
German-owned railway in Shantung Province. Furthermore, on January 18,
1915, the Japanese government secretly presented twenty-one demands to Yüan
Shih-kai as head of the Chinese government, while the Western powers were all
occupied with their own fighting in Europe. These Japanese demands embarrassed Yüan Shih-kai terribly for they would make China virtually a dependency
of Japan. But his shrewdness kept Japan at bay until he died at fifty-six.

When World War I had gone on for three years, the American government
severed diplomatic relations with Germany and invited the neutral powers, including China, to do the same. This caused much dispute within the Chinese
Republic then in the hands of various war lords. China eventually joined the
Allies in name without being able to send troops to the battlefields. When World
War I ended, the Versailles Peace Conference gave no decision in favor of
China's regaining her rights over the German possessions in Shantung against the
claims of Japan. At the same time Japan had not lessened her pressure on China
for the twenty-one demands. On May 4, 1919, a great mass protest broke out in
Peking, originating at Peking University. Though the ruling war lords tried to
quell the demonstrators by killing students and professors indiscriminately, this
May Fourth Movement soon spread from Peking to the entire country. The city
of Kiukiang, where I was born and lived, was no exception. Together with many
other middle school students in the city, grieved and angered by the unreasonable
Japanese demands and the injustice of the great powers at Versailles, I raised my
flag of protest and joined in the mass demonstration day after day.

This May Fourth Movement could be regarded as the great turning point in
twentieth-century Chinese history and it was also the first "cultural revolution,"
for it not only roused much of the Chinese populace to become aware of their nation's future but it also set the thoughts and culture of her young people moving
in a new direction. At that time the old classic style of writing was transformed
into a vernacular expression, making it much easier to read and understand. No
change took place in the writing of the Chinese language; this change was in the
grouping of words and choice of vocabulary. But the difference was as great as
the change from Chaucer's English into modern American newspaper style.

When I left home to enter the National Southeastern University in Nanking in
1922 there was a powerful movement urging all young Chinese to study the
sciences, for "only science can save China." It was felt that all China's ills in
recent years could have been cured had we known enough science to produce
modern machinery and military equipment. Like many other freshmen, I took up
the study of chemistry in the hope of doing something to save China in the future.
In those days, China had a number of science professors who had all been
educated abroad, mostly in the United States and England, but unfortunately the
science departments of most universities had not all been equipped with modern
laboratories. Professor Chang Tzu-kao, (now ninety-one years old, whom I saw
in Peking in May 1975), initiated me into the study of inorganic chemistry and

physical chemistry. After four years I earned a B.Sc. degree. As there was no possibility for me to do advanced study on the subject in China then, I tried to win a scholarship for studying abroad, but failed.

In 1924 General Chi Hsieh-yuan, the war-lord governor of Kiangsu Province whose headquarters were in Nanking, waged a terrible civil war against a neighboring war lord, the governor of Chekiang Province, General Lou Yung-hsiang. Each regarded his respective province as his own property and fell upon the other without paying any heed to the so-called central government in Peking. Our university in Nanking could not be opened for classes and all the students were disbanded for a term. I took this opportunity to travel to Canton where my elder brother, Chiang Ta-chuan, was working as chief secretary to the head of the Kiangsi army, Li Lieh-chun.

In those days China's so-called central government was in Peking in the hands of war lords. It could only exercise its power over a very limited area, though it was recognized as the legitimate government by the foreign powers. Dr. Sun Yat-sen, as the first provisional president of the Republic of China (in 1911), had set up a similar government in Canton, opposing the one in Peking, with five southwest provinces under his control. Though Kiangsi Province was not included, the former strong man of the Kiangsi army, Li Lieh-chun, had brought all his men to support Dr. Sun. So had the head of the Hunan army, Tan Yen-kai, and many others also gathered in Canton. As Dr. Sun Yat-sen realized that his early failure was due to the lack of a sufficiently strong force, he set up a military academy at Whampoa and appointed as its head Chiang Kai-shek who had recently returned from army training in Japan. As this academy was brand new, it created a new spirit in the air of Canton and many young men rushed to enroll in it. Many of my brother's friends advised me to join instead of going back to Nanking to continue my studies. However, my brother agreed with me in not wishing me to waste my three years' university study. But the civil war was still raging around Nanking and I could not return there yet.

A friend of mine had opened a summer school on Hainan Island and asked me to join him. So I went without hesitation, for I never missed a chance to travel whenever I could. I arrived by boat at Hai-k'ou harbor, Chun-shan, and was met by my friends from the old German-built consulate, now returned to China. Hainan Island is the southernmost soil of China, known in Chinese history since the Han dynasty. The famous Sung poet-statesman Su Tung-po was governor there for many years. As it is a good-sized island some thirty miles from the mainland, the provincial government of Kwangtung at Canton had control over it, but it was always administered by an army general. Before World War I, the French sought to annex it to the French colony of Annam, for it is close to Haiphong. But the British thought it was in their sphere of influence in south China and did not agree. Therefore Hainan remained Chinese territory.

There were many minority people living there and I saw a few with tattooed faces, arms, and bodies like those in Africa and New Guinea. Right in the center of the island stands a big mountain called Wu-chih Shan or "Five Finger Mountain"; most of the natives live around there. Only a very few Chinese go into that area. I tried to learn much about the island's general structure, natural resources, and products during my months' stay and I returned to write a long article on it which was published in the popular magazine, *Tung-fang-tsa-chih,* of Shanghai in 1924. That was my first piece of writing to be published. I still feel happy whenever I think of this first publication of mine.

My family's financial position had deteriorated with the general economic condition of the entire country. The influx of cheap foreign goods from Japan and other countries was killing the native trade and prices for daily commodities were soaring. After the death of my grandmother, my uncle and aunt did not manage the family affairs well and fairly. I was therefore unable to go abroad to study with the family means. With a mere B.Sc. degree and an elementary knowledge of science I could do nothing but teach. I accepted a teaching post in the eleventh middle school in Haichow in the northern part of Kiangsu Province.

Haichow is quite close to Shantung Province, near the eastern coast of China where Po Hai, the Yellow Sea, lies. The land is rocky and rugged as well as mountainous and rice could not grow there. Because of the lack of transportation in those days, rice was quite expensive there and the school cook could not afford to give us rice every day. Now and then I managed to eat one or two *wo-wo-tou,* a very dark-colored solid bun or small bread loaf made partly of wheat but mixed with a little corn and chaff and some grass roots. Most peasants and people of the place ate this kind of *wo-wo-tou* almost daily. But some could not have even this to eat. I encountered many beggars when I walked outside the school. I soon learned how poor my fellow countrymen could be in other parts of the country, particularly in the north.

After six months I was recalled to teach in my native city of Kiukiang, south of the Yangtze River. By then the war lords in the north were quarreling terribly and fighting against one another even more intensely than before. Dr. Sun Yat-sen's provisional government in Canton decided to take the advice of Mikhail Borodin, the Russian representative sent by Stalin, to co-operate with the rising Communist Party of China. In spite of Dr. Sun's untimely death, the Canton provisional government decided to send a combined northern expeditionary force to destroy the war lords in Peking and appointed General Chiang Kai-shek as the commander in chief. Borodin even promised to provide funds for party operations, with the Soviet government underwriting most of the expenses, and also to provide training officers for the military groups. (Before the northern expeditionary force marched out of Canton, Chiang Kai-shek sent his elder son to study in Moscow.)

With a number of Russian advisers, the combined northern expeditionary force had great success and reached Nan-ch'ang, capital of my province of Kiangsi. At the command of General Chiang Kai-shek, the former system of provincial government had to undergo a complete reform and reorganization.

Many young, hot-blooded men (including me) became excited at the sight of the new force and the prospects of new programs for the future. In a matter of days I was appointed a member of the newly set-up Provincial Educational Committee to discuss a new educational system. After a closed session of the committee, some secret quarrel emerged among the leadership from a hidden struggle about the coalition between the two parties, the Kuomintang and the Communists. A strong member of the Educational Committee, Tuan Si-peng, was entrusted with the organization of an "A.B. Tuan," or "Anti-Bolshevik Group," and asked me to join it. I rejected the invitation immediately, for my aim was to contribute my best effort to do what was good for our country, not to enter unnecessary quarrels before all the war lords had been liquidated.

I decided to express my patriotism in another way and joined the newly created northern expeditionary force led by General Pai Tsung-hsi setting out for Shanghai and beyond. I traveled with a regiment under the command of Captain Chen Lei from Nan-ch'ang to Shang-jao, then Chiang-shan, Chin-hua, Lan-ch'i, Chuchou, and finally Shanghai via Hangchow. We did not have to fight all the way, for the rice soldiers of the war lords just laid down their rifles when their leaders escaped or disappeared. We were well received as their saviors by the local people at each place.

After a few days in Shanghai, the regiment I belonged to was dispatched to conquer Soochow, while another general, Cheng Chien, led his army to take Nanking, long a national capital like Peking in Chinese history. It was a very important city, and close to the great commercial and industrial center of Shanghai. General Chiang Kai-shek immediately moved his headquarters from Nan-ch'ang to Nanking. With the support of many veteran followers of Dr. Sun Yat-sen's, such as Hu Han-min, Wang Ching-wei, Tan Yen-kai, and Li Lieh-chun, a new central government was set up in Nanking which was soon recognized by the Western powers and the so-called central government in Peking automatically lost its significance. This caused the northern war lords much confusion.

As General Chiang Kai-shek was still the commander in chief of the entire national army, he was virtually the head of the government, though not yet in fact. He did not like the presence of General Cheng Chien in Nanking, for the latter was known to have leftist inclinations. He soon disappeared without trace. And General Pai Tsung-hsi, under whom I came northward, belonged to a Kwangsi military group which had not always been in agreement with General Chiang Kai-shek's movement and which was much feared by the latter when General Pai reached the important city of Shanghai. Should General Pai Tsung-hsi be allowed to move further northward his army could easily smash the much-confused northern war lords and his power, together with that of the Kwangsi military group would have been much enlarged. Fearing he would be unable to control him afterward, Chiang Kai-shek stopped General Pai Tsung-hsi from pushing his army northward any further.

I stayed with my regiment in Soochow with nothing particular to do for a month or so. Out of the blue one day I learned that an unbelievable purge of Communist personnel from the army and government had been staged in the night from Nanking. The political adviser of my regiment, Wang Er-tso, a Communist and graduate of the Whampoa Military Academy at Canton, disappeared and someone told me that he had been shot. Many Commknist personnel were killed over night and many escaped to the headquarters of the Chinese Communist Party high up in the mountains of Kiangsi Province. It was then suggested that I take the place left by the political adviser, temporarily, until a definite appointment came from Nanking; but I declined.

After another month in Soochow, I got away to Shanghai where my elder brother Chiang Ta-Chüan was now working as the chief secretary to the military governor. The latter's authority did not include the Shanghai International Settlement where foreigners enjoyed their extraterritorial rights. This extraterritoriality had long been a sore to all Chinese who felt that China could no longer be regarded as an independent country. It meant that after China was defeated by the English and French, the unequal treaties ensured that foreigners and their activities in China were subject to their own laws—not Chinese law. It left foreign merchants and missionaries, their goods and properties, and to some extent their Chinese employees, converts, and hangers-on, all immune to Chinese authority. This was a disgraceful imposition of the Western powers upon the Chinese, and yet the newly established central government in Nanking needed the recognition of these powers and raised no objection to the extraterritorial treaty.

When I reached Shanghai, I became one of the unemployed. Unexpectedly one day I met, on a trolley-bus, a former university mate of mine, Dr. Yen Chi-tzu, who had just returned from France to take up the post of dean of the School of Sciences and Engineering in the Chinan University at Chen-yu, Shanghai. On finding that I was without a job, Dr. Yen asked me to join his department and teach inorganic chemistry. I felt greatly relieved.

Just at that time, the Japanese who had long regarded north China as their sphere of influence and had also been working and plotting with a number of noted collaborators to set up a puppet government in Peking, sent a regiment to occupy the city of Tsinan, capital of Shantung Province. This naturally agitated the Nanking government and angered the Chinese people. The Japanese commander, General Fukuda Hikosuke who occupied the city of Tsinan, demanded a meeting with General Chiang Kai-shek for direct negotiation. This was absurd, since General Chiang Kai-shek was the virtual head of the Nanking government, as the Japanese knew very well. It would not have been proper for him to meet a commander of a small regiment from a foreign country. So a great-uncle of mine on my mother's side, Tsai Kung-shih, who had studied in Japan some years before, was appointed as special envoy to negotiate the withdrawal of the Japanese army from Chinese soil.

My great-uncle came to Shanghai to see my brother and ask if he could take me with him as his aide. As I had to get leave from the president of my university, it was arranged that I should follow the delegation by train early the next morning. Most horrible news reached us about eight hours later. As soon as my great-uncle and his party reached Tsinan station on May 3, 1928, they were savagely murdered by the Japanese before they could even set foot in the city. It was obvious that the Japanese did not want the incident to be settled locally. Having murdered the entire party, they denied that they had ever seen them. How could a foreign army illegally stationed on Chinese soil kill a Chinese envoy like this? Where was the international law? It could happen simply because the central government at Nanking was so very weak. However, I had not been able to join my great-uncle's party that day and so I am still alive.

After six months of teaching in Shanghai, I was appointed head civil servant of Wuhu County in Anhwei Province. Without much delay, I got the permit to leave and caught a river steamer to Anch'ing first and then to Wuhu. In those days China was divided into twenty-eight provinces and each province had some ninety or more *hsien*. A *hsien* is something like a county in America or England, though some are even bigger than an American county. For convenience I use the term *county*.

Each county government was headed by a civil servant appointed by the provincial government; they also had judicial duties. After the Opium War, many Westerners came to China and had dealings with local government officials; they translated the Chinese term for the leading official of a *hsien,* or county, as "magistrate." To me a magistrate only deals with legal matters, nothing else. But the Chinese head official of a *hsien* had many more duties to perform. He generally controlled four departments, though some had an additional department concerned with legal problems. The first department dealt with general affairs, chiefly social welfare, and included a police bureau and military headquarters; the second dealt with land taxes and other financial matters; the third with local educational matters in conjunction with the local educational bureau; and the fourth with housing problems, the construction of public roads, and so forth as well as the special building bureau. Some bigger counties might have a special local court to deal with legal matters. Otherwise the local county government could perform legal duties with the help of an assistant lawyer or judge appointed by the provincial government. In other words, the head civil servant of a county government in China had many duties to perform, for he was a welfare manager with hundreds of policemen and an even larger number of soldiers in his charge; a tax collector for the national treasury; an educator in charge of the whole county's schools; an architectural and engineering administrator in charge of all the public works; and he could be a judge in the county court as well. Though he would be assisted in all matters by the various bureau heads who were appointed by the provincial government, he had to be able to meet anything that arose with alert and sound decision. He was certainly much more than a magistrate.

The head civil servant and the four bureau heads as well as the assistant lawyer were not elected by the local people but appointed from above. This was where the Chinese political system could easily go wrong if the provincial governor and other higher officials based their choices on personal favor rather than ability. As a matter of fact this Chinese political system is centuries old, originating with the Han Confucian scholars about the third century B.C.; it has varied only slightly from period to period. Though each new dynasty was set up after great disturbance and unrest among the people, most noted Confucian scholars of each period rose to join the new government to run the whole country with their bookish minds blindly following the traditions. They seldom tried to alter the land-tax rules, and they never tried to educate the masses. Confucius's teaching (Confucianism) has been praised by similarly bookish-minded Western scholars in their writings and teachings in the universities, none of them realizing that Confucianism, totally unlike Christianity, has never been discussed in seminars or preached to convince those who disagreed. The Confucian teaching prevailing in my term of office was no different from that of the early days of the Han dynasty. I had to struggle against many odds.

On the first day of my arrival at Wuhu, I met all my subordinates and the various bureau heads, many of whom had been working in that local government for years. They knew that I had been in the army and also had gained some experience in my brother's office when he was a local governor in two different counties. They dubbed me an ultramodern young man, for I was eager to alter their traditional practices. At that time, although the central government had been set up in Nanking, the whole countryside was far from peaceful. It was infested with many kinds of evildoers: robbers, thieves, and bandits. The new Nanking government had no policy for helping or protecting the people, or for providing work for the starving masses; therefore, numerous able-bodied youths in their early twenties ran wild and robbed innocent people unless they could be enlisted in the army as rice soldiers.

As so many criminal cases occurred, my immediate task was to organize protective groups in the bigger villages and country towns to safeguard the peaceful lives of the people. I had to gather the local elders and country gentry for discussion. Funds had to be raised for a technical institute to feed and train the poorest young men, I suggested. The idea was immediately rejected as being a slow process which could not solve the acute problems. So all decided to follow what was known as 保甲制度, *Pao-chia chih-tou,* or the "guarding villages program." This program had been established long ago; in it the whole population was to contribute money to buy old rifles. These would be issued to groups of ten or more men in each village and town. The group would be led by one of the gentry or rich landlords. I detested this organization for I thought that those with their old rusty rifles and no training might do more harm than good to the people. However, the organization was approved by the higher authorities. I could do nothing to reverse the decision.

At that time the Nanking government was under the leadership of General

Chiang Kai-shek who, as mentioned, had no intention of destroying the power of the remaining war lords in the north. He could not yet ask the whole country to elect him as president of the Republic, for many elder persons who had long associated with Dr. Sun Yat-sen such as Hu Han-min, Lin Seng, Wang Ching-wei, Tan Yen-kai, Li Lieh-chun were still alive and active. Instead, Chiang Kai-shek tried to entice these war lords with new high posts if they would change their loyalties and come over to the Nanking government. The local military governor of my county, Wuhu, General Yueh Wei-ching was one of those remnants.

One early morning, my chief of police reported to me that his men had caught three robbers stealing money from a local bank along the main street. I naturally told him to send the robbers to my court to be tried and sentenced. No sooner had I given my order than a telephone call came from the military governor asking for the robbers to be transferred to his headquarters, an order which I could not very well refuse. At heart I was confident that he would give them a severe punishment. Instead, he sent the robbers, who happened to be his soldiers, to be stationed in front of the very bank they had robbed. Their presence scared all the people in the bank as well as its customers. No Western journalists appeared in my county to record this—a small matter in a huge nation like China. But can my Western readers imagine such a chaotic situation to be possible in China around 1929? And what a position I was in then; I could do nothing to protest, for the local military governor was a war lord who would not heed my words. Actually there was no need to have a military governor in my county, but General Chiang Kai-shek placed him and many others in the bigger cities in order to surpress any uprising of the people against him.

Several months later, another general, Pao Kang, came to replace General Yueh Wei-ching as the military governor of Wuhu. It was understood that General Pao Kang's appointment came from the headquarters of General Chiang Kai-shek. It was not long before this general joined in a secret plot with another former war lord, General Shih Yu-san, to overthrow the Nanking government, aided by the most powerful old war lord, General Sun Chuan-fang. While they were preparing to assault Nanking, General Pao Kang sent several hundred of his soldiers to beseige my *yamen* (my head office and official residence) in the hope of carrying me away or seizing money from my office, for the local governor was also a land-tax collector. However, the attempt to retake Nanking failed and I became free to go on with my work again. Despite all the upheavals during my term of office, I survived. I used to patrol the countryside on horseback with a number of my soldiers to give assurance to the people. It did have some effect. At the same time, I learned more about how our people actually lived and suffered.

The neighboring county, Tan-tou, was not only much troubled by robbers and bandits but also by the evil-doings of its governor. I received an order to go there and investigate the peoples' complaints. Afterward, I was transferred to replace the bad governor. I had great trouble in putting affairs in order there and also had to borrow many soldiers from the local military governor and lead them over the countryside in a pacifying movement. Tan-tou County was not on the shore of the great Yangtze River but on a strong tributary. Within a month of my taking up the local governor's post there, in the monsoon period of July 1929, a torrential rain fell suddenly and the river water inundated thousands of acres of rice fields and left thousands of peasants homeless. The Yangtze River and its tributaries had not been dredged for centuries. I had to organize refugee camps and raise funds for food, all of which was a heavy task. While the rescue work was being carried out, I sent a petition to the provincial governor asking to have the river dredged and some irrigation work done. This was immediately turned down

Old China's way of irrigation.

without a moment's consideration. I could not understand why and was greatly disillusioned.

In May 1930 I was recalled to Kiangsi Province and was appointed to take up the local governorship of Kiukiang County, my birthplace. This was something unusual for, by a long tradition, no one was appointed to govern his own birthplace, for fear that he would give favors to relations and friends. This is just the opposite of the Western democratic system of election by the local people. Kiukiang is situated on the south bank of the Yangtze River as is Wuhu County. But Kiukiang is a key city between Hankow and Shanghai and also the main outlet for the products of several provinces. After China was defeated by the Western powers, Kiukiang was made one of the treaty ports.

There was a short stretch of shore along the Yangtze River which became part of the English and Japanese concessions and where the Chinese were not allowed to sit on the public wooden benches. When I was a young boy of eleven, I used to walk with my grandfather along the riverside. Once my grandfather, at seventy-five, feeling rather tired on the walk, sat down on a bench for a little while, but the concession policeman came to drive us away. Though young, I became very angry at this unreasonable treatment in my own hometown. After that I seldom set foot in the concession in my city. Under these abominable and unequal treaties enforced by the victorious Western powers, the incompetent Manchu rulers had not only assigned many land concessions to the foreigners but also gave them the extraterritorial rights which caused endless trouble to the Chinese. Whenever a Chinese rascal committed a crime he just ran into the foreign concession area and no Chinese policeman could enter to arrest him. Foreigners also had the right to sail their gunboats and big cargo ships right into the heart of China.

The English and Japanese concessions in Kiukiang had been abolished by our foreign minister, Chen Yu-jen, in 1926 before I returned to take up my new post. However, the bad, old memories were still there. Much of the best land in the city of Kiukiang was owned by foreign missionary bodies on the understanding that they would build schools and hospitals but there was to be no construction for business enterprises. This law the missionary bodies did not follow, yet no local people raised any protest. This indirectly caused much hardship to many of the city dwellers.

Both Wuhu and Kiukiang Counties had a county court to deal with important legal matters, especially criminal cases. So I was free of that there, but this had not been so in Tan-tou County where I dealt with all legal and criminal cases with the help of a lawyer appointed from the higher court in Anch'ing, the capital of Anhwei Province. In Tan-tou I had the power to dismiss some of the leaders of the civil-defense groups in the various villages when they abused their power with the firearms they had acquired. I also dealt with three rare cases of divorce there. By rare I mean that the Chinese women under the Confucian tradition were in such a low position and so submissive, that they would hardly dare ask for a divorce, even from the worst kind of husband. Since divorce was considered so shameful, I tried to persuade the husband against it if possible, for the wife would not be able to get work and would be greatly despised by all who knew her. In the West people have heard much praise of Confucian principles, but they ignore how the later Confucianists twisted Confucius's words to give all the advantages to men so that they could take three or four wives while a woman would not be allowed to remarry if she became widowed.

The first case that came to me in Kiukiang to be dealt with was a dispute about a piece of property between a missionary school and a Buddhist monastery. The local military governor who was on good terms with the principal of the missionary girls' school, suggested to me (actually instructed me) that I had better give the land to the missionary school. My reply was that I had to study the case carefully and, in fact, I eventually sent the case over to the local court for judgment. This displeased the local military governor and was the beginning of severe friction between us later on.

In Kiukiang I then tried to do something for the reform of our land-tax system. Though the local governors were also land-tax collectors, they never had clear records of the taxes for the whole areas under their control. The exact records were in the hands of a number of individuals who had inherited the privilege of tax gathering from their forefathers. From my experience in the two counties in Anhwei Province, I realized that the entire economic system of China relied chiefly on the land taxes levied all over the country—a system which had not been questioned or analyzed since the Han dynasty, about the third century B.C. These real-estate tax collectors had their appointments renewed by each new local governor, who had to rely on the old hand to get the money for the local functionary as well as for sending up to the higher authority. These collectors had absolute security in their jobs which were never questioned or examined. They often overcharged the peasants even taxing them double or triple because they were too ignorant to realize that they should get a receipt for what they had paid. The Chinese peasants on the whole were holders of some land, not more than two or three acres; they struggled to get enough to eat and to feed their offspring, not to mention enough to pay a landlord's rent as well as the government tax. This caused the peasants terrible hardship year after year. It puzzled me at the time why the newly established government at Nanking had not tried to probe into the evils of the old Chinese land-tax system, but let it go on and on as before. I had had a modern training in scientific method, so I wanted to tackle this problem as far as it lay in my power.

I first tried to compel the tax gatherers to let me have the actual records of the land taxes for the whole area. They all refused. I continued to put pressure on them and kept them under surveillance for six months but they still showed no signs of yielding. I knew they thought a new governor would soon come to take my place. At the same time I sent a long report to the higher provincial government in which I suggested having the whole area under my jurisdiction photographed from the air in order to work out the exact holding of land, so as to calculate how much tax should be collected. When my memorandum reached the provincial head and his subordinates, it caused nothing but derision. I was branded as a mad young man.

All this time, the Japanese never ceased intriguing to get north China under their control. Although they did not officially send their army to occupy the territory under the eyes of many other nations, they worked out one plot after another and eventually carried off the former young emperor Pu Yi, who had abdicated in 1911, to Manchuria and set him up as the puppet-emperor of Manchukuo—a kingdom for the Manchus. This in fact cut China into two nations; naturally, the Chinese people became greatly enraged. The Nationalist central government at Nanking sent a strong protest to the League of Nations at Geneva, for they could not dispatch troops north to check the action. After much argument and evasion among the representatives at the world body, a fact-finding group of important diplomats from many nations, led by an Englishman, Lord Lytton, arrived in China.

After having spent some months in north China and Manchuria, and since there was no air link with Geneva from Peking in 1931, they traveled by train to Hankow and then stopped over at my county, Kiukiang, to board a river steamer for Shanghai. I received the news from our representative, Dr. Wellington Koo, whose secretary wired me to prepare twenty cars to take the whole delegation up the famous Lushan mountain for a sight-seeing expedition. I asked my police chief to find the cars, but at the end of the day they had found only five, including two old track-lorries. Kiukiang is not a big city and most people walked about it. Though there was a possible road up to the bottom of the mountain, it would not be easy to bring all the delegation up a four-thousand-foot-high mountain in a short time.

However, I planned a good banquet to entertain the delegation. After the feasting, I rose to give a toast and made a brief speech begging the fact-finders to consult their own consciences in passing a sound judgment on the facts they had observed in north China and Manchuria. Lord Lytton, returning the toast for his group, made a few remarks about what they had seen in the north and said that they would have a final discussion in Geneva. The Englishman was a well-known diplomat and knew what to say to small local government officials. However, my speech, rendered into English by my secretary, was recorded in full in the Shanghai Chinese newspapers—*Sheng-pao* and *Hsin-wen-pao*. Someone told me later that the Kiangsi provincial governor, my immediate superior, was not pleased at my making the speech, but I had in fact invited him to Kiukiang to lead the reception; however he had not replied.

Unfortunately another great trouble befell me during my term of office at Kiukiang in connection with a powerful Nationalist army general, Tan Tao-yuan, whose soldiers were stationed in Kiangsi Province directly under the control of General Chiang Kai-shek. To my great surprise, his chief of staff came down from Nan-ch'ang one morning to call on me in Kiukiang. He told me how a certain captain of their army, in charge of an army unit of about two hundred soldiers, had been shot dead in Kao-an County, several hundred miles away inland in the western part of Kiangsi Province. His soldiers had been accompanying the captain to headquarters with a truckload of money for the army pay. They had turned on their captain and killed him and then divided all the money among themselves before running away. Though the Nanking Nationalist government had already been established for five years, they had not yet taken up the task of building roads for better transportation and no inland banks could handle large sums of money. So an army unit was always sent to guard a large sum of army pay whenever it was to be transported from one place to another. The chief of staff said that since Kiukiang was a treaty port with many roads and river communications, all these soldier-robbers must have come to Kiukiang and deposited the money. He demanded that I, as the head of the local government, should recover all the money for his army.

This was a thunderbolt to me. How could the Kiukiang government be held responsible? I asked him. It was the captain's fault that he had no control over his men. The chief of staff became angered by my retort and declared forcefully that if I, as head of the Kiukiang government, would not help, he would send soldiers all around the countryside to find the lost money. This kind of childish behavior would have amazed any Westerners, had they come to hear of it. At that time most Western journalists were praising the newly set-up Nationalist government in Nanking, but they failed to realize how little control the Nanking government had over its army leaders who, in fact, differed very little from the former war lords.

As soon as I heard that soldiers had actually been dispatched to my countryside, I immediately sent a telegram to the head of the Kiangsi provincial government, my immediate superior, asking him to stop the unwarranted movement of General Tan's soldiers. No reply came. The soldiers had been searching in every peasant's home, upsetting their lives and robbing them as well. How could a so-called modern republic have such a situation with soldiers robbing innocent people under their general's orders? Did the commander in chief, General Chiang Kai-shek, know this? I grieved the whole night over my helpless effort to save our people from suffering; instead they were suffering still more under my administration.

Though disillusioned, I still persevered, hoping I could save a few of my fellow countrymen from suffering while I was in office. But nothing turned out as I imagined. Some twenty miles away from the city of Kiukiang there had long existed two big oil refineries, owned by the Asia Shell Company and the American Standard Oil Company. They must have been built there after Kiukiang became a treaty port years ago. In 1931, the American Texaco Oil Company wanted to build yet another refinery there. The representative of Texaco had plenty of money at his disposal and must have got hold of many corrupt middlemen, compradors as they used to be called, who received commissions from both foreigners and Chinese. The company's representative came to Kiukiang and had evidently spent enormous amounts to buy a piece of land for the new buildings. They had bribed people from the Kiukiang Chamber of Commerce down to the junior staff in my office without my knowing anything about their transactions. When the commissioner of my building bureau sent an application for the construction for my sanction, I immediately questioned how the Texaco Company could have bought the land. I secretly probed into the matter and found that one of my staff had played a great part in the fraud by stealing my official seal to stamp the deed. I eventually managed to get this false deed back to my office for cancellation.

These goings on naturally produced a turmoil in the city. Everybody who had had a share in it feared arrest and having to pay back the money they had already squandered. Of course the powerful Texaco company applied for assistance from the American embassy in Nanking, and their ambassador communicated with the Chinese ministry for foreign affairs. At the same time, what had happened became a good opportunity for the local military governor, who had no friendship for me, to run me down as hard as possible, saying that I had received huge sums in the land transaction with a foreign company and this would endanger the safety of our country. Soon I received a reprimand from the generalissimo's headquarters and another from the minister for foreign affairs, Wang Cheng-ting, in Nanking. Naturally this did not please the head of the provincial government, General Hsiung Shih-hui. I was summoned to Nan-ch'ang to face a direct rebuke from General Hsiung. My defense was that the Texaco company should have tried to negotiate for the land directly with my office instead of working through so many dishonest agents. Their representative who must have heard many stories about Chinese cunning and inscrutable ways had started to use bribery to get hold of the land. General Hsiung had nothing good to say for me and thought of transferring me to another place. I asked him for a fair judgment of what had happened in this matter as well as in the case of General Tan's soldiers going round the countryside robbing the people at will. My superior became enraged and I parted from him deeply depressed about my intention to do something for the people. Eventually I came to the decision to relinquish my post.

The real problems of China lay with the masses of the population who were illiterate and did not know that they had the right to be well treated and well fed and not to be molested as they always had been. In order to understand their own human rights they had to become literate. This was the biggest task that any Chinese central government has had to face. The high officials of every succeeding dynasty in the past, all old Confucian conservatives, had ignored the masses who were the backbone of the nation. In addition to this, Chinese officials of the past never put their minds to planning the nation's finances as a whole; as far as I could remember the central government in Nanking did not once work out the annual budget in any year. Most of the officials just knew how to squeeze money from the people for themselves.

The bulk of the Chinese peasants lived in the countryside far away from the towns. They themselves had no means to get education and they could not afford to send their children to school even if the schools had been nearby. In all three counties where I was head of the local governments I went to talk to the peasants face to face whenever possible and tried to do whatever I could for them. They all told me that their children had to walk miles to get to the government school and they had to return for meals. There were no such things as school buses or free milk and lunches for children. I found many peasants' living conditions appalling and pitiful. Many had no land to till and no work to do but had to beg in the streets and country lanes. I made a number of suggestions for raising money to feed them but they were always turned down by my superiors. I could not understand why the Nationalist government in Nanking did nothing to help the peo-

An old peasant telling of his past suffering.

ple. I became sadder and sadder. Whenever I saw a beggar on the road, nearly dying of starvation, I remembered the famous lines by the great poet, Tu Fu of the T'ang dynasty more than a thousand years ago: 朱門酒肉臭路有凍死骨, "Chu-men chiu jou hsiu, Lou yu t'ung-szu ku," which can be translated as follows: "Within the vermilion gates wine and meat growing rank; But on the roadside the bones of those frozen to death." The words described conditions so many years ago; how was it that our people could still be suffering in the same way in the twentieth century? It proved that none of the governments, in the hands of so-called Confucian scholars, in the past had done anything for the common people. The Nanking government officials, though supposedly equipped with modern and new ideas, did nothing new but simply were carrying on the old ways.

To have quarreled with a powerful general, my immediate superior, could mean a lot of trouble for me in those days. I was now in a great dilemma—how to find work to do. Even going back to teaching had become impossible. I confided all my troubles to a former schoolmate and good friend, Lo Ch'ang-hai, who had won a scholarship to study in England four years before. Lo replied immediately in a long letter of more than ten pages. As a student and scholar of political science, Lo urged me to find a means of leaving China as soon as possible. I thought this over again and again, for I had the uncomfortable feeling that the new war lord might cause me more trouble. I also wondered how I could go to

England knowing so little English. Though I had learned some English terms in my study of chemistry, I had almost forgotten even these after a few years in the army and civil service. Then there was the difficulty of finding sufficient funds for the traveling expenses and for living. Many people thought I must have accumulated a good deal of money after serving as head of the local government in three counties. It was the general practice to accept heavy bribes during one's term of office. I was young and had taken the posts with the avowed aim of wiping out the past social evils. After I relinquished my post, I had little and could just manage to keep myself going for a short while.

I then discussed the matter with my elder brother who had always been very kind to me from my childhood as an orphan and who had helped with my education and seen me through the university. He was grieved at the unfortunate situation I had got myself into, but he did not reprimand me for resigning the post. Eventually he said that he would help and ask some of his friends to help, too, if I could gather some funds together myself. After two months of preparation, my brother saw me off at Shanghai on a French liner that would take me to Marseilles, whence I would continue to London. (Alas, I was not to see my brother again.) I felt quite eager to go away and quite confident of what I might gain in this trip, but it was an indescribable torture to leave my invalid wife and a family of four young children, the youngest of whom was only a little more than a year old. The means I had would only be enough to keep me, living modestly, for a year or so, thus there was no way of taking my family with me. And my brother- and sister-in-law promised to look after them. Only experienced political exiles can understand what I went through.

On the French liner I spent thirty-three days hardly uttering a word except to a young cousin who traveled with me and who was going to study law in France. When I reached Marseilles, I found my friend Lo Ch'ang-hai had sent a telegram to the boat welcoming me and instructing me how to take the train to Paris and then to proceed from there to London. I reached London on June 15, 1933. I had the joy of seeing my good friend, and my life outside China began.

In England

MY FIRST TASK on reaching England was to learn the language so as to make my way in those totally new surroundings. With my limited means I could not afford a highly qualified tutor. I just picked up whatever I could by listening to the conversations around me and reading the news in the daily papers. What struck me most forcibly about England was that everybody could read and write, while this was not so in China. All expressed their feelings very freely and clearly, unlike the majority of my fellow countrymen who were illiterate and thus inarticulate. I was also struck by the term *common man* which the English used frequently and unrestrictedly. What they meant by *common man,* I soon understood, was those people who were not aristocratic or government officials or university professors. The ordinary English people ate their breakfasts, lunches, and dinners just like the aristocrats and officials, though the dishes may have been simpler. Most of the Chinese masses had nothing in common with their superiors; many did not have a proper meal for days or any proper clothes to wear at any time.

It was my good fortune to be introduced to Sir James Stewart Lockhart, a retired British commissioner to Weihaiwei in China and also a former governor of Hong Kong, who could speak Chinese fluently. He was the author of a book entitled *A Manual of Chinese Quotations* with Chinese text which was published in 1903, the year I was born. In our conversations he often quoted phrases from the Chinese classics which I had learned by heart in my school days. This made us firm friends. He asked if I cared to give lessons in Chinese at the School of Oriental and African Studies at London University, since one of their lecturers—a former missionary in China—had just died. I seized this offer at once, for not only would the little income be a help to me, but also in teaching the students I would learn more English. After a few months' work, I began to make more friends and was invited to a number of places.

One day I received a strange but interesting letter from a Captain St. John Baker, the founder of a society called Men of the Trees. The society was dedicated to the protection of trees and to afforestation where planting was especially needed. To spread information and raise funds an exhibition of paintings of the world's trees was to be held in London in 1934. Captain Baker had been told by the Chinese legation that I was one of the Chinese in London who could paint, so he got in touch with me for a painting of Chinese trees. My father had been a painter and I had learned the technique from him when I was between ten and twelve. I had left China in haste and was not properly equipped with painting materials, but the legation halped me to find a Chinese brush, ink, and some Chinese semi-absorbent paper.

Though bamboo grows in many countries, it is always regarded as a plant particular to China, for Chinese painters have loved to paint it. So I made a painting of Chinese bamboo for the show. To my great surprise this spray of bamboo was reproduced in the *London Evening Standard* on the opening day. This inspired me to try my hand at some other paintings and I soon did a number of birds—ducks, swans, and seagulls—in St. James's Park as well as in Kew Gardens in Surrey. One of my duck paintings was reproduced in the *Illustrated London News*. I received a few letters afterward commenting on the reproduction of my work. One of the writers was the late Sir William Milner, who had great interest in things Chinese, particularly Chinese porcelains and paintings. He asked if he could come to see me. Eventually we became good friends. I was then invited every year to spend some time with him at Parceval Hall, a sixteenth-century mansion he owned in Yorkshire. Later on I stayed at Cluny Castle in Aberdeen, Scotland, and Pekenham Hall, Ireland, and several other well-known mansions and country houses.

While enjoying my stay in those various beautiful houses, I realized that many Englishmen with means preferred to live deep in the country. They had their telephones and cars to make connections with the city whenever they wanted. There was no division between town dwellers and countryfolk. This was another point of contrast with China, where town dwellers disliked going to the country and often looked down on the countryfolk as being ignorant and illiterate. As a rough generalization I can say that the urban Chinese of my childhood and youth were mostly able to read and write and lived comfortably while, as they received no education, the countryfolk were largely poor, ignorant, and hardly aware of anything going on outside their small plot of land and hut. The countryfolk had a sense of inferiority and were always shy of talking with town dwellers, which tended to make the latter arrogant, haughty, and snobbish toward them. The children of the town dwellers were rarely encouraged to go and see the countryside and were absolutely ignorant of what a rice field looked like and of how the rice they ate every day was grown. I recalled my experiences in the offices of local government, how I had two different types of people to supervise and how much this added to the complications of government. I resolved then that if I ever went back to the same sort of post in China I must try to even up these two different groups of people. The best way would be to educate the countryfolk so that they could communicate with the town dwellers on an equal footing.

Toward the end of 1934, two noted Chinese painters, Professor Ju Peon (Hsu Pei-hung) and Professor Liu Hai-su, each brought from China a good many contemporary Chinese paintings for exhibition in London and other cities in Europe. I was asked by them to lend a hand in the arrangements. The interest in Chinese art was growing considerably at that time. A great writer on Chinese painting, the late Laurence Binyon, keeper of antiquities at the British Museum, together with a number of well-known British collectors of Chinese art, such as George Eumorfopoulos, Neill Malcolm, Oscar Raphael, and many others, made direct arrangements with the Nanking government to hold an International Exhibition of Chinese Art at the Royal Academy of Arts in London from November 1935 to March 1936 and the subject came up in the news daily.

Many London publishers took the opportunity of commissioning books on Chinese art to coincide with the opening of the exhibition. A young director of Methuen & Company, J. Alan White, had the idea of finding a Chinese artist to write such a book; this, he thought, would give an additional attraction to it. My name was suggested and a meeting was arranged. I had to confess that my knowledge of English would not be adequate for writing such a book. Alan White was not discouraged but urged me to jot down my ideas in Chinese first and then translate them into my rough English just so that he could understand my points and from this rough draft he could get the book edited and published. Just at the time, one of my young students, an Oxford graduate, offered to do this editing job for me; this would make the task easier, for she had learned Chinese from me. She worked hard polishing my clumsy English and questioning me on this and that aspect of Chinese art in general, and painting in particular. Alan White read the edited manuscript with approval and sent it to press at once. This started me on my writing career outside China—something I had never dreamed of.

The book, *The Chinese Eye,* an interpretation of Chinese painting, was first published on November 21, 1935, just before the opening day of the International Exhibition. The book sold well and had to be printed twice within two months. From this book I won more friends; many collectors of Chinese art were interested in it. Alan White, who became one of my best friends in England, encouraged me to keep on writing and so I brought out *A Chinese Childhood, Chinese Calligraphy,* and many travel books. The little income I got from the books, together with teaching, kept me going without worries and at the same time I tried to send some money back home to China. Unfortunately the Chinese government did not have a sound policy in economic management and the exchange of foreign currency into Chinese dollars at the official rate was terribly low.

Though I intended to return to China in 1936 or 1937, the news of the Japanese movements and infringement in north China caused much unrest among the Chinese. Eventually the Japanese staged a full-scale invasion, pouring in a great army to occupy the whole of north China. The Nationalist government in Nanking with the commander in chief of the Chinese army, Generalissimo Chiang Kai-shek, had made no preparation to resist and could not resist the sudden attack. Most of the army, which originally belonged to the old war lords but had defected to Chiang's camp, was very weak and just retreated from one place after another.

My elder brother sent me news about the family from time to time telling me not to return yet.

The Japanese, moving fast from the north, soon crossed the Yellow River to reach Chengchow, capital of Honan Province. The nationalist forces were not strong enough to meet the Japanese and Generalissimo Chiang Kai-shek ordered them to bomb the dyke of the Yellow River (Hwang Ho) to let the water out and stop the oncoming force of the Japanese. They bombed the dyke, without telling the local people to evacuate first. Thousands of innocent countryfolk were drowned while the Japanese had no losses, for they changed their tactics and went round another way to reach central China.

The rebuilt banks of the Yellow River at Hua-yuan-kou, Chengchow, filling the gap made by the Nationalist army in 1938.

In the spring of 1938, my native city Kiukiang was swiftly occupied by the invading force. Our old family house, built more than a hundred years ago, was soon broken into and torn down by the Japanese soldiers. My brother had to take our entire family up to Chungking, a hilly city of west China, in the wake of the retreating Nationalist forces. He died soon after reaching Chungking. The grief inside me, like a knife cutting little by little, was utterly indescribable and for many days I felt it unbearable to go on living.

After endless sleepless nights worrying about the rest of my kinsfolk, realizing that mere worry would not help them, I tried to concentrate my mind on some useful activities. I read more English books, mainly travel books about China. I found these books unfair and irritating at times, for they laid stress on such strange sights as opium smokers, beggars, and coolies. I could not deny that these existed, but it seemed to me that those writers were pandering to an un-healthy curiosity in their readers and the publishers accepted them knowing that they would sell well. So an idea arose in my mind to write about what I saw in London and other places on the principle of looking for similarities among all kinds of people not their differences or their oddities.

While I was still feeling terribly grieved at the loss of my most beloved elder brother and also worrying about the rest of my family, some English friends urged me to go away somewhere for a holiday. In the end I was advised to go to see the English lakeland where some of the English poets had lived, for my friends knew that I read English poetry. I reached Wastwater first, then some other lakes, and ended up at Derwent Water. At the sight of the green hills, trees, and water, so different from the London houses and streets, my mind became clearer and my feelings relaxed. I took notes about my daily wanderings and made some rough sketches in Chinese ink.

Upon my return to resume my teaching at the School of Oriental and African Studies, the manager of a publishing company came to see me and asked me if I could write a book about my experiences in London, for he remembered seeing the reproduction of my painting in the *Illustrated London News*. Happily I showed him the notes I had made about my holidays in the lakeland together with the ink paintings I had done there. He looked at them without much comment, saying the work would be slight and could not sell too well. Besides, no one would be able to understand a Chinese painting of English lakes. I said that if these would not make a salable book, how could I spend the time writing some-thing about London. He then promised to take the material back to his office for consultation. The next morning he rang me up saying that they had had a board meeting and decided not to take the book. I then let other publishers have a look at it but it was turned down by them also as being too thin. An introduction to two more publishers brought no better result. So I did not pursue the matter any further.

However, six months later, the first publisher came to ask me about the Lon-don book again, whether I would care to write it. My answer was negative if they did not think the little book about the English lakeland worth their while to publish. After another month's delay, he came to say that they had decided to take the risk of publishing the slight book on the English lakeland, with one con-dition—no royalty. This made me think for several days but I finally agreed that to have six complimentary copies of it was better than nothing. So he took the manuscript and drawings for printing. Another trouble was that they objected to my using the title *The Silent Traveller in Lakeland*, for they thought ''The Silent Traveller'' sounded sinister. I laughed and suggested that it would make the book sell better. However, the English publisher was very cautious and careful, in case it might induce inquiries from Scotland Yard: Why does a Chinaman want to walk silently? Many English people at the time had not forgotten about Dr. Fu

Man Chu. Eventually we came to a compromise—to call the book *The Silent Traveller: A Chinese Artist in Lakeland.*

The late Sir Herbert Read was kind enough to write a preface in which he said, "Mr. Chiang has dared to enter our national shrine and to worship there in his own way." The book was published first in 1937. To everybody's surprise the small first edition sold out in a month and the publisher asked for a reprint, telling me that times had changed. So I got a change too—in the shape of a normal royalty. Since then my books on London, the Yorkshire dales, Oxford, Edinburgh, Dublin, Paris, New York, Boston, San Francisco, and Japan, were successively published as a Silent Traveller series.

Though I tried to ease my own worries by writing something light, my head became heavy at times, for war rumors over Europe were spreading fast, putting everybody, particularly the English who had enjoyed peace for twenty-five years, into a state of nerves. Following the Munich affair, a temporary peace reigned until the Germans invaded Poland. Then the English prime minister, Neville Chamberlain, declared war against Germany on September 3, 1939.

At the time of the declaration I was having dinner at a friend's house and when the black-out was announced, the young son of twenty and a daughter one year younger became quite hysterical, trying to pull down blinds again and again. The young man expressed great fear of being called up for fighting, while the girl felt that she would find it difficult to face the war conditions. I never realized that war could affect people so violently, for I had been through so much fighting in China and could not understand why a Western war should be so different from ours. After two or three months, the whole country was on a wartime footing and nobody showed any hysteria any more for war had become a fact. Air fights and air defense were a great feature of this war. The English Air Ministry sent up hundreds of big silvery balloons high above London to intercept the enemy and protect the capital—actually the focus of the world at the time. From BBC broadcasts I heard about a thousand German planes flying over the British Channel and five hundred English fighter planes going up to engage them in combat, before they crossed the English Channel. Many German planes were shot down almost every day. Some managed to get through, though they had to fly high above the net of the silvery balloons, for a plane would burst at once if it touched a ballooon. I could not help admiring the English way of air defense which seemed so effective then. From time to time I got up early and went out to watch the dog-fights in the air and saw one or two planes burst into flames like fireballs on several occasions.

On one occasion a bomb fell directly on the house in Parkhill Road, Hampstead, where I had lived for several years. The bomb exploded late at night and the top part of the house was smashed to pieces, while the ground floor and part of the second were left in a mess. It was a time bomb. As I was the occupant of the second floor, many neighboring friends and some of the home guards went to dig in the debris after the explosion in order to find my body. None of them knew that I had gone to Oxford to give a talk on Chinese art for the Chinese Society there that night. My landlord found out where I was and sent me a wire about the bombing. I returned to London the next afternoon, but the train track was also bombed and it took me more than three hours, instead of only one, to reach London. I met my landlord and we went to see the bombed building. A notice prohibited anyone from entering the dangerous place. Though I could see the small back room of my flat was still there where I had my paintings and material such as brushes, ink, and paper, I could not go to retrieve them.

London in winter got dark very early, soon after four o'clock, and the German planes would start to reach the city after five. I could not go back to Oxford the same day, for I was doing some translation work for the Ministry of Information, but I had nowhere to stay either. At the kind suggestion of the woman who used to clean my flat daily, I spent the night at her house—a basement flat—just opposite mine. She told me that we all had to sleep under the staircase as instructed, for it would be safer. Though I heard bombs dropping at times that night, nothing happened to us and I walked out the next morning to finish my business.

Everybody carried on business as usual, despite the air bombing every night from five till the next morning at six. It was a terrible strain for every Londoner. The undaunted spirit of the English, old and young, won my great admiration. One day a main water pipe was bombed, so there was no water supply. I saw people washing their faces with the cup of tea they had gotten at a mobile canteen where some old people, seventy and eighty years of age, were in charge. Another day I came down from Oxford and spent the night under the staircase in my neighbor's basement again, but she could not provide a meal for me with her scant rations. I had to walk to a nearby restaurant, by Belsize Park Underground Station, after dark. There was only one other customer eating there with four waitresses and a cashier. We heard bombs being dropped here and there at times and our dishes shook a little too. After having something to eat and on my way back to the basement, I saw far in front of me a live fire bomb coming down. I knew what to do and laid down on the pavement immediately. The explosion must have knocked me unconcious for several hours until the drizzling rain wet my clothes and brought me around. I discovered nothing had happened to me and walked to the house where the woman received me kindly with a hot cup of tea.

After the bombing had made my flat uninhabitable, I remained in Oxford where my landlady was very kind and let me move in the few things remaining from the wrecked house and stay as long as the war lasted. I was later called back to London to sign a claim for damages which would be paid after the war ended, but when I met the officer, I said that since I had not lost myself, I did not want to sign for any other damage. Many people in the office thought I was stupid and foolish, but I smiled at them and went away. In my own mind I praised the English system of looking after the people so well and with such consideration, while I recalled that the Nationalist government in Nanking had made no attempt to check the black market which had soared to the highest point and was simply robbing the people.

I also heard how the sons of my good English friends who had been called up had been killed in battle or died in the air fights. They were from well-to-do families and one was an aristocrat. I also heard that the son of the English foreign minister, Anthony Eden, had been killed in air-training exercises. All English young men were subject to conscription to defend their country and many went to war willingly with the resolution to defend not only their country but also Western civilization. Ever since my childhood in China I never feared that I would be conscripted in time of war. Even when China had been at war with Japan, more fiercely than ever, none of the rich men's sons had been called up, or the sons of any government officials; they were sent by hook or crook to study in America. The Nanking government under Commander-in-Chief Chiang Kai-shek fought the war against Japan with rice soldiers who had no training to meet the modern weapons of our enemy. Failure and constant retreat were inevitable. All this made me furious at the behavior of the Nanking government and even more worried about the whereabouts of the rest of my family, whether they were still in Chungking or not. I had had no news from them since the death of my elder brother.

Unexpectedly the Japanese bombed the American fleet in Pearl Harbor. Soon hundreds and thousands of American G.I.s poured into England; many of them were stationed around Oxford. A most curious and strange event happened to me at this juncture. After the considerable success of my first book *The Chinese Eye,* I thought I should try to introduce the art of Chinese calligraphy to the West, as it was completely unknown then. Many of my friends advised against it, for they said the subject was too obscure and no Westerner would be interested or understand it. However, Alan White fully agreed that I should try, though he warned me again and again that the book might have no sale. He and I sat together and discussed each point of the subject as I wrote it, and he spent much time rendering my expression more explicit for Western readers. Eventually the book *Chinese Calligraphy* was completed and published in the latter part of 1938. Indeed, it had little sale on publication, for this was the time of the Munich Agreement. Its sale dwindled to nothing after war was declared against Germany in 1939. As the war reached its height in 1940 and 1941, London suffered much from bombing and people were intent on getting food and clothes rather than books. Very few toys or Christmas goods had been manufactured in the past three years. But when the American G.I.s began to land in England, not too long before the approach of Christmas, they bought up all the copies of *Chinese Calligraphy* to send home as Christmas gifts. This was most curious and strange to me, for I never had the idea that my writing could be a seasonal present.

As China had been at war with Japan, one of the Axis powers, since 1937, President Franklin D. Roosevelt insisted on including China as one of the Western Allies, with the approval of Winston Churchill of England and Joseph Stalin of Russia. Not long afterward, the English foreign minister, Anthony Eden announced the abolition of extraterritorial rights in China. This made the Chinese, particularly the young ones, wild with joy. On the day after the announcement, the Chinese Nationalist flag was raised together with the English, French, Russian, and American flags in Piccadilly Circus. China had long been looked down on by Western eyes and there were never good words for her in the newspapers. The raising of the Chinese flags was regarded as a most unusual event, at least in the minds of the Chinese. I especially went down to London to walk about near the Chinese flag all morning and afternoon like a young child.

Soon after this, an international P.E.N. conference was held in London and another Chinese friend and I were chosen as China's representatives. In the morning of the opening day of the conference, the American writer and novelist, Thornton Wilder, flew in to represent his country; Dr. Salvador de Madariaga represented Spain and H. G. Wells and a few others represented England. At the first meeting I sat beside Wells and Madariaga and had a good talk with Wilder who told me that his father had been an American diplomat in Shanghai for a number of years and he had spent his young years there. We then paid a quick visit to Bernard Shaw and I made a sketch of him for the comic painting I later created of him being gripped by a black girl from an account in his book *The Adventures of the Black Girl in Her Search for God.* I thought the girl did not find God but Shaw instead. This painting was an illustration in my book *The Silent Traveller in London,* which was published in 1940.

Directly after the collapse of France, General Charles de Gaulle, with many of his army personnel and followers, came to London to set up a provisional government and work out plans for retaking France after the Axis should be defeated. He was soon followed by Emperor Haile Selassie of Ethiopia after Benito Mussolini had occupied his country. A provisional government of Ethiopia was set up along the same lines as the French. They both worked out details for retaking their countries when the time should be ripe.

I kept wondering if the Chinese Nationalist government which had retreated to Chungking had made similar plans for retaking all the lost territories when the Japanese capitulated. I even asked the Chinese embassy in London about it, but they had no idea. It seemed that the Chinese Nationalist government had no hope of ever defeating the enemy. At that time Chungking had no air protection, for the Chinese air force was nonexistent. Whenever the Japanese planes flew over to attack Chungking, the whole population had to hide inside the mountain caves and could only come out when the Japanese planes had dropped all their bombs and flown off. In the meantime, the Nationalist government had no way of controlling the soaring prices of daily commodities and inflation went from bad to worse. The black market was resorted to for everything and many poorer people could not afford to buy anything to eat, but simply waited to die. The Chinese currency became almost valueless, just like the German mark after World War I.

A small amount of rice cost thousands of Chinese bank notes. Life was unbearable except for those who were already rich or who had ways of going through the black markets. Chinese soldiers learned to retreat, though many died fighting. Many lost their ammunition and weapons. The Americans, regarding China as an ally, poured in aid in money as well as supplies flown over the Himalayan mountains, as I was told by an American friend of mine, Lieutenant General Frederick Atkinson, who was in charge of supplies and flew over the mountains many a time. But the American people did not know that much of their ammunition was lost too.

At last the war in Europe had almost reached its last phase. London was still holding out undauntedly, although everybody there, including the officials— apart from Winston Churchill—had grown weary. The Germans had lost so many of their pilots and planes in air fights with the British that they devised pilotless gliding planes which they sent off the French side of the English Channel to bomb London. After the pilotless gliding planes proved ineffective, the Germans invented the doodlebugs, V1 and V2, which were shot over to London blindly and killed many people indiscriminately. I was told that one would be all right if he heard the sound of the doodlebug being dropped, otherwise he would have gone with it. However, the Germans, though clever in applying scientific inventions, could not fight on against the combined forces of the English, French, Russians, and Americans. Finally Hitler and Mussolini came to bad ends. After signs of weakening could be detected, the American president Harry Truman resolved at the eleventh hour to employ the atom bomb on two Japanese cities. That immediately brought about the capitulation of Japan and the war for Europe, America, and Russia ended in 1945. But it did not end in China, though all Japanese soldiers had laid down their arms on Chinese soil.

The Chinese Communist army had taken part in the fight against Japan and had achieved a number of victories by using guerrilla tactics. Thus much of northern China was in their hands, which did not please Generalissimo Chiang Kai-shek. At the time of the Japanese capitulation, large areas from Shanghai southwestward were left for the Nationalists to take over. Many officers were sent down from Chungking to occupy the land, but few of them had any administrative experience; some, I was told, were personal servants who had served the wife of the Generalissimo for years. These officers reached Shanghai, Nanking, and many other places and behaved like vultures, trying to seize big pieces of meat from the local people. At first their arrival was joyfully welcomed as if they were saviors, but no sooner had these Chungking officers set up their offices than they began to arrest people one after another as collaborators with the Japanese and then demanded large sums for their release. This went on day after day and roused great hatred among the local people—it was no better than being under the Japanese. The result was that many were driven to escape and join the Communist armies or at least to give them help. The Nationalist government, on returning to Nanking, had no support from the people and could not restore its administrative control.

Just at that time, Generalissimo Chiang Kai-shek decided to hold the so-called nationwide election and he was elected president with General Li Tsung-jen of the Kwangsi military group elected vice-president, which he never expected. This shows how different the Chinese national election is from an American one. The so-called nationwide election in China was not a one-man-one-vote affair, but only those connected with the government were allowed to vote. Strangely enough, the nomination for president had caused no opposition, but that for the vice-president had. Generalissimo Chiang Kai-shek had planned to have Sun Fo, son of Dr. Sun Yat-sen as his vice-president, but the result came out differently. He was furious with the people who had helped to work out the election.

The Communist army had gained much experience in the guerrilla warfare against the Japanese, while the Nationalist army with their rice soldiers, had no idea about fighting. So the inevitable outcome befell the Nationalists. When the Communist army reached Shanghai, quite close to Nanking, Generalissimo Chiang Kai-shek made the decision to escape to Taiwan. Though General Li Tsung-jen intended to make a stand, Chiang Kai-shek withdrew his soldiers and took them with him. General Li could not fight empty-handed.

In his book, *Present at the Creation*, Dean Acheson, the late secretary of state, had the following passages:

> In addition to the aid given by U.S. Forces, China Theatre, in redeploying the Chinese armies and repatriating the Japanese, by the Marines in North China and by the U.S. advisory group, the United States provided from V-J Day through 1948 approximately a billion dollars in military aid and a similar amount in economic aid.

Again:

> On the day that I assumed my office Generalissimo Chiang Kai-shek resigned his, turning the Presidency of the Republic over to the Vice President, General Li Tsung-jen. Before doing so, however, he transferred China's foreign exchange and monetary reserves to Formosa and requested the United States to ship military equipment destined for China to Formosa. This left General Li without funds or a source of military equipment.

Dean Acheson was very clear about some things but he did not realize that Chiang Kai-shek had not resigned his presidency but would hold onto it in Taiwan all the years till his death.

As soon as the Nationalist government was transferred to Taiwan and no longer had a footing on the mainland, the British government recognized the new Communist government in Peking and this action was followed immediately by the Indian government. This was a natural outcome, for Taiwan is less than one-fiftieth of the area of China.

I thought the transference of the Nationalist government to the small island of Taiwan was a political move lacking in foresight and very unwise if it hoped to survive. Many of the so-called great politicians with the Nationalist government never had any idea of working out a plan to regain control of the whole of China which they could suggest to their leader. In fact they were all *chih cheng-chih-fan ti*, 吃政治飯的, "rice politicians," just yes men who wanted to secure their own survival for as long as possible.

But the real reason for the failure of the Nationalist government was that it never cared for its people; instead it caused them more miseries year after year. In the end it discarded its people altogether, except that small number of rich ones who could afford to move to Taiwan and those others who could get there by hook or crook. Though Dean Acheson did not probe into the basis of the Nationalist government's failure or ever succeed in understanding the background of Chinese politics, the following words of his expressed the general attitude toward China at the time:

> Many, I continued, bewildered by events in China, failed to understand the background, looked for the esoteric cause, and charged American bungling. No one in his right mind could believe that the Nationalist regime had been overthrown by superior military force. Chiang Kai-shek had emerged from the war as the leader of the Chinese people, opposed by only one faction, the ragged, ill-equipped, small communist force in the hills. Chiang controlled the greatest military power of any ruler in Chinese history, supported and given economic backing by the United States. Four years later his army and his support from within the country and outside it had melted away. He was a refugee on a small island off the coast.

The above is a very much generalized, sweeping statement, but one which represented the ideas of most of the Americans at the time. There are many disputable points in the statement.

The Chinese Communists did start with a very small force, not well-equipped and with none of the advantages of help by any powerful outsiders. But their leaders, small in number, were all devoted patriots with the aim of reviving China as an independent country with a sound economic base to support all the Chinese masses. Though their army was small and ill-equipped, it gradually became bigger and better equipped—by the American military supplies lost to them by the Nationalists. However, the Communist leaders had their greatest and most powerful fighting weapon in the wholehearted support of the people, for the people knew that the cause for which the Communist army was fighting was theirs. Wherever their armies went they got full support and help from the local people, whereas when the Nationalist army appeared, the people ran away as fast as they could. Though Dean Acheson described Chiang Kai-shek as controlling the greatest military power of any ruler in Chinese history, he was the ruler in name only, he never managed to gain control of the huge power of the Chinese people. The people are the backbone of any nation; no one can be regarded as a good ruler unless he wins the full support of the people. The whole-hearted support of the people is the only weapon that can win the struggle; mere military might cannot. (For instance, the great military might of the United States is known the world over, but it failed to achieve its goal in Vietnam, simply because it had no support from the local people.) The soldiers of the Chinese Communist army were taught why they had to fight and for what they fought, and this brought victory. The Nationalist army, mostly rice soldiers, did not have any idea of their goal and many of them were persuaded to go to the Communist side. Generalissimo Chiang Kai-shek was doomed to become a refugee on the small island of Taiwan, for he lost the support of the people.

Taiwan is an island directly opposite Fukien Province. It had taken a most heroic stand for the Ming dynasty against the intruding Manchu conquerers of China. It was there that the hero Cheng Cheng-kung, whom the Japanese called Coxinga, waged war against the Manchurians when they tried to overthrow the Ming dynasty. Though he won many battles, he later was overwhelmed by the great odds and had to retreat to Amoy. He finally drove the Dutch out of Taiwan where he established himself as king. He died on May 1, 1662, at the age of thirty-eight. His life story had been told in French and in Dutch. In Japan it is particularly known through a play called "Kokusenya Kassen," or "The Coxinga Battle." Whenever we Chinese talk of Taiwan's history the name of King Cheng Cheng-kung is always brought in. However, Japan defeated China in 1894 and took Taiwan in 1895. Just before the end of World War II, President Roosevelt, at the Cairo Conference, suggested the return of Taiwan to China after the war. The Chinese Nationalist government eventually took control of the island after Japan's capitulation and made it a province of China in 1946. The first provincial governor, an army general appointed by the generalissimo, exercised an iron hand over the local people who revolted and many were killed. Afterward the generalissimo came with his big army, followed by a good many rich families from Chungking and Nanking. They soon began to lord it over the local people. And it was obvious that the two groups could not see eye to eye with each other.

III

In America

AFTER THE END of World War II in Europe many of my books were sold in America and I gained a number of good readers who became my friends. I was then invited to come to do a book on New York and also one on Boston. I managed to secure a berth on the first reconditioned British Cunard liner, the *Queen Mary,* in 1946 with three thousand passengers, but only eighty men including me as the youngest. The rest were G.I. brides with seven hundred babies. It was the experience of a lifetime on that liner; I will never forget how one baby began to cry and immediately was followed by hundreds of others. I stayed in New York for six months, then went back to London to write my book *The Silent Traveller in New York* which was published in both London and New York in 1950, though it was printed in England.

After my return from my first visit to New York, I found out that my sister-in-law and three of my four children had made their way back to our native city Kiukiang. They were living in a rented house with their long-bedridden mother. (My wife had contracted an incurable disease before I left China in 1933.) She and my elder daughter and son were being looked after by my sister's grown daughter and my younger daughter was being cared for by my sister-in-law. My second son, quite young, had joined the Nationalist army and gone to Taiwan. Though relieved to know where they were, I thought more than ever of what to do about the children. In 1947 I managed to get my elder son to England to study at the London School of Printing, for he did not know enough English to enter an English university. He graduated after three years' study and went to work in Jersey, one of the English Channel Islands. Later he married a Jersey girl and they have two children. I wanted to get my second son out of Taiwan, but found no way to do it.

I still had no opportunity to return to China, even for a short visit. And, as the little royalty I could get from my English publications was not enough to live on, I expressed my wish to come to New York. My good friend Dr. Louis M. Hacker, who was then dean of the School of General Studies at Columbia University, and Professor L. Carrington Goodrich, chairman of the Chinese and Japanese Department, had found an opening for me to give a course at Columbia in 1955. This was a reason for me to live in New York; but, at the same time, it involved me in another complication: The new central government in Peking was at loggerheads with the United States government, and in 1956 America was swept by the fear of "un-American" activities under the powerful Senator Joseph McCarthy. I dared not even mention my kinsfolk in China, nor could I express my wish to see Peking.

In this situation it was even difficult for me to travel to other countries. After having taught in Columbia for a number of years and finally becoming a permanent member of the staff, my future in the United States seemed to be assured, so I became an American citizen. With the American passport I tried to go to Taiwan to see my second son who was still in the army, but my application was not accepted. I did not understand why I could not go in as a China-born Chinese. However, the American passport enabled me to travel to South America, the Caribbean, the Mediterranean; to Italy and Turkey as well as Greece, the Black Sea, Japan, Southeast Asian countries, Australia and New Zealand, New Guinea, and a number of Pacific islands such as Tahiti and Fiji. My idea in traveling so widely was to pursue the principle of finding similarities among all people throughout the world. Though I could not stay long enough in each country to learn all about the lives of other people in detail, I feel that nowhere has there appeared a type like our Chinese war lords who could kill and rob others without any provocation.

The time arrived for my year's sabbatical leave from Columbia, 1966–67, and I took it without hesitation. I worked out a round-the-world trip, including a stop in Taiwan for three days, intending to persuade my second son to come to America to study. I had no difficulty in obtaining visas from any country except Taiwan. I then asked my friend, Dr. William Royall Tyler, formerly assistant secretary of state, then ambassador to the Netherlands, to intercede for me with the American ambassador in Taiwan and this produced the visa without further delay. I saw my second son, Chien-fei, and his wife, Chiao-wen, and a baby girl, San-san, and told them to book passages on a boat to the United States via Japan. A month later I met them in Yokohama, Japan, and they reached Boston before I returned from my world trip. They were well looked after by my friends, Dr. and Mrs. Walter M. Whitehill of the Boston Atheneum, for a month before Chien-fei got work at the Meriden Gravure Company to learn printing. This worry of mine was at last settled.

From time to time I got news of my two daughters. They began their studies after Kiukiang and Kiangsi Province had been taken over by the new central government. Both girls were well treated; the younger one graduated from Wuhan University and got a teaching position in Peking, where she now lives with her husband and two sons. I have felt at ease since then, and have tried to send a little money to them from time to time.

Since I was a China-born Chinese, it was inevitable that I should occasionally be asked questions about China by Western intellectuals and others. I also occasionally took part, by request, in some seminars discussing Chinese topics. I was not always happy to participate in such gatherings, for it seemed to me that some of the speakers who were noted specialists on China's political history and who made sweeping judgments on events in which I had actually taken part some thirty or forty years before did not see the situation quite clearly. So many books on modern China have been published, particularly on China before 1949. Though a few of the writers seem to appreciate China's acute problems, on the whole they touch points seen only from the outside; they do not penetrate the real Chinese life. Only a few years ago the late secretary of state, Dean Acheson remarked that no Chinese governments in past centuries had succeeded in feeding all China's millions and they were still not able to do so. This was a rash statement, yet it touched the deepest problem that China had and still has. Just imagine, the Nationalist government never did anything to find out how to keep its people fed properly.

A question which I was frequently asked by many young American students who majored in Chinese or Japanese studies at Columbia University is why

An old teacher of Ta-chi-chuan, an ancient Chinese system of health exercises.

China did not succeed in becoming modernized as Japan did. The following passage from my book *The Silent Traveller in Japan* offers my explanation:

Emperor Meiji was the Japan-born god and all his ministers were Japan-born citizens. Their voices easily reached the ears of all Japanese, who followed their instruction as if they were god's words, without the slightest hesitation. Emperor Meiji had not only a great aptitude for acquiring a knowledge of the Chinese but that of the western world as well. He had the wisdom to accept the ideas of others and to co-operate with them. Many rulers in the course of history failed to become great simply because they were too stubborn and narrow-minded. Under the great liberal-minded ruler Emperor Meiji, many able men had the opportunity to advance their ideas with imperial support and as a result Japan has become a great modern nation.

In contrast it was obvious that China could not undergo any reformation like Japan. The emperors of China never thought of doing anything for the people's good because they were in constant fear of being overthrown by the people they governed. This is because China's rulers since the seventeenth century were not Chinese but Manchurians. They never trusted the Chinese people from the time they took over the throne in 1644 and, suspicious of any movement started by the Chinese, they would crush it instantly without inquiring what it was all about. The emperor kept himself deep inside the enormous palace grounds in Peking and his voice would take weeks, even months, to reach the regions in the south and other remote areas of China. Even if the people heard, they would not obey without force and any kind of reform was impossible. The cruel treatment meted out by the Manchurian rulers was shown in the *Literary Inquisition* of Emperor Chien Lung (1772–88) when many innocent Chinese men of letters, who had committed not the slightest offence, were killed.

I need not quote more than this. One can imagine that any Chinese who wanted to import the Western idea of democracy to let him have his say in government would be beheaded instantly. Most Western diplomats and journalists who were stationed in Peking probably never knew about the Chinese literary inquisition and I would urge those going there now to read *The Chinese Literary Inquisition* by Professor L. Carrington Goodrich. Many were the cases when one or two words, harmless in themselves, were treated by the Manchus as implying a criticism of them. Not only would the writer of those words be beheaded, but also his whole family and his friends as well. When did the Chinese know freedom of speech or even thought? How could China become modernized like Japan as long as we had those cruel rulers of non-Chinese origin? I therefore had reasons for my devotion to Dr. Sun Yat-sen's three Principles of the People; he tried hard to dethrone the Manchus.

I have mentioned the incompetent Manchu rulers of China in a few passages already. I should like my readers to consider how, when the British started the Opium War, the Manchu rulers had their soldiers oppose rifles and guns with ancient Chinese spears and swords. How could China not be crushed and forced to surrender? In the days of the Boxer Uprising they had the unreasonable belief that the human flesh of Chinese soldiers would not be pierced by Western bullets and cannon balls. That was why young Chinese born some sixty or seventy years ago had to suffer the indignity of the unequal treaty granting extraterritorial rights and concessions. In my book *The Silent Traveller in Edinburgh* I mention the following incident:

During the last Manchu dynasty a Chancellor named Mei Shou-chi accompanied Chinese envoy H. E. Liu Chih-tien to France and England, and afterwards returned to see the Minister of State, Chi Shih-yin. After introductions, the latter said: 'You must have endured great hardship during more than four years on the terrifying waves. Aren't you happy to see land again?' Mei replied: 'The journey from China to England took little more than a month. After that we went ashore and did not go back to sea until the mission was completed.' Chi Shih-yin was astonished to learn that there was land in England and inquired whether there were also dwelling houses and edible crops as in China. Hiding a smile, Mei answered. 'Yes, indeed.' Chi Shih-yin smiled and said: 'Now, I have learned something new. I used to think of our envoys as generally living on board ship the whole year round and seeing no land at all. Now I know I was mistaken.'

That was only a little more than eighty years ago. How ignorant could a minister of state be? And how could people like him change China into a modern nation?

My good friend, Robert Payne, in his book *Chinese Journal,* wrote;

> During the reign of the Ch'ing dynasty (Manchu dynasty), Sir Robert Hart asked the Emperor's Prime Minister what he thought of the western influence in China. He replied, 'You are all concerned with waking us up and setting us off on a new route; you will succeed in doing it, but you will regret it, because once we are awakened and set off, we will go faster and farther than you think, and a great deal more rapidly than you would like.'

Perhaps the answer was truer than the prime minister knew.

Many high government officials in the central government set up in Nanking by the Nationalists in 1928 were educated abroad, chiefly in America, and they knew well what the Western countries did for their people. Strangely enough few of them tried to make much use of their studies or else their voices had never been listened to. However, their knowledge of English helped them to climb higher in position merely because they could be used to communicate with the Americans who were backing the Nationalists. The Taiwan government hangs on as long as America backs it. At this juncture, Taiwan is not a free land because the Americans have at least five thousand soldiers stationed there. Why so? I don't know.

In the spring of 1972 the news of President Richard Nixon's arrival in Peking made a stir throughout the whole world. Many rejoiced about it, but others did not. However, from that time on, contact and traffic between China and the United States opened up. From the second half of 1972 on, hundreds and thousands of Westerners and overseas Chinese eagerly applied for visas to go to China and many did in fact spend some weeks there. Desperately anxious as I was to go to see my family, I still did not rush to apply for a visa. I noticed that those Chinese who managed to go at that time were mostly scientists like Dr. Yang Cheng-ling, Dr. Lee Tsung-dao (both Nobel Prize winners in physics), Dr. Wu Chien-hsiung, Dr. Yuan Chia-liu, Dr. Lin Chia-chiao, Dr. Wang Hao, and a few others who were educated in China before 1946 and who now hold high teaching positions in American universities, together with many overseas Chinese from Hong Kong and Southeast Asian countries. Most of the Europeans and Americans also went in groups as scientists or scholars in some special subjects that the new central government of China in Peking would like them to investigate and for which she could provide interpreters. My reason for going there would be different, for I am a China-born Chinese with a number of kinsfolk left during years of absence; so I had to suppress my agitated feelings and wait for a better opportunity to send in my application.

After 1945 I had had news of my two daughters through Hong Kong friends. I learned that they both had married and become schoolteachers. Neither of them had had any idea of what I looked like until I sent them some small photographs of myself. I cannot find words to describe my heartbroken state of mind at times. Only those who have endured a similar situation would understand. Nevertheless, my own strong will to keep life going and my unwavering belief that we should meet again in the long run had helped to make the waiting easier.

Directly after my retirement from Columbia University in July 1971, I received an invitation to teach a year at the Chinese University of Hong Kong. Unfortunately I could not begin to teach until January 1972 and I therefore did not try to apply for a visa to go back to China to see my kinsfolk. As soon as I arrived in Hong Kong to start my teaching assignment I was invited to teach at the Australian National University at Canberra for the year, 1972–73. I never expected these invitations after my retirement; as they had come, I could not very well decline. So I could only delay my application to return to my homeland for a visit.

Before I decided to send in my application for a visa on my return to New York from Australia, I tried to read and hear about the reactions of those who had recently come back from a China visit. They seemed to fall into three types. Among the first were many of the overseas Chinese-American intellectuals (China-born Chinese who came to the U.S. when they were young) who now hold good positions in American universities, government, or big business concerns. This group of visitors to China was chiefly American-educated. I may be wrong in assuming that some of them knew little about China's countryside life, but I can be quite sure that they were all originally town or city dwellers, for they must have had a solid educational foundation before they could win a government scholarship or they must have had family means to go abroad for advanced studies. Living in cities or towns, they buried their heads in books and had little chance to understand what life was about in the city itself or in the countryside. Now they had their higher education, in highly developed countries like England, France, and America and enjoyed full modern facilities. Being well-educated people, they would be greatly interested to see the China of the 1970s, though there would not be much left of the China they knew when they were youngsters. At times, no doubt, they remembered how they used to live in those days, with many servants and all kinds of comforts which their wealthy families could provide and plenty of money to do what they liked with. Life in present-day China would seem to them somewhat restricted in comparison and lacking in luxury.

The second group was composed of overseas Chinese, many of whom had been born and bred outside China. They were not very different from young Englishmen, Frenchmen, or Americans. Their knowledge of China and her history went no deeper than some oddments of information they had gathered from their parents and relations. They went to see the present China in a mood of curiosity. Something typically Chinese in fashion or manner which they did not know before roused their interest to some extent, but when they looked at the ordinary Chinese houses and other amenities, their thoughts immediately turned to London, Paris, or New York for comparison. Their unfavorable impressions could often be gathered from their talks and writings. I had a typical experience of this when I stayed in the International House near the University of Sydney, N.S.W. Australia. While I was dining with a number of students, a girl of Chinese parentage, who had been born in Kuala Lumpur, Malaysia, told her companions how she had gone with a group to see the new China, but they had no skyscrapers, nothing really new at all, only small one-story houses everywhere.

The third group were largely European and American intellectuals, young and old, experts on particular subjects, who went to see the present China partly out of their need for new material and partly to compare the reality with what they had heard about or studied. Quite a few of them had been employed in Chinese studies and had read many books by Western scholars and also had heard lectures on Chinese civilization from Chinese and Western professors. This group quickly became disappointed if what they found was not up to their expectations.

I read some writings by all these groups after they returned with both favorable and unfavorable comments. I could not join the scientists nor medical experts who went to China either by invitation or by arrangement to investigate special subjects. Nor could I rank myself with any of these three groups of visitors. My thirty years of life in China before 1933 as well as my personal experiences as the head civil servant of three big counties put me into a rather different category as a visitor to the present-day China. I would undoubtedly compare what I could see now in China with what I knew of her before 1933. This would be inevitable and was why I held back and waited for the right opportunity to travel far and wide in my homeland again.

Off to China at Last

SHORTLY AFTER RETURNING from my teaching assignment at the Australian National University in Canberra, I thought the time might be ripe for me to apply for a visa to revisit China. I wrote to the Chinese Liaison Office in Washington in March 1974, asking for an application form but received the reply that there had been too many applications for visas and no more forms were to be sent out for the time being. This was a setback; it seemed there was no opportunity for me yet.

However, a few months later came a telephone call from an old friend, Hou Tung, with whom I had studied in London in 1934 and who had now finally located me in New York. He had come to the United Nations as an economic adviser to the Permanent Mission of the People's Republic of China. He had been working in New York while I was teaching in Australia and got my telephone number through a mutual friend. I couldn't place him when I first heard his voice on the phone, but when we met we discussed our days in the lodgings we had had near one another in Camden Town, London, and revived old memories of the times we had spent together. This happy meeting with an old friend whom I had known some forty years ago inevitably reminded me of how even more enjoyable it would be if I could see my own daughters after forty-two years. So at our third meeting I expressed my wish to go back to see the new China, my longing to see my family, and my hope to travel around my homeland by myself rather than in a group. Hou explained the difficulties: so many people now wanted to go to see China and the facilities and accommodations were not yet adequate for all their needs. That was why only a limited number of visas could be issued at a time. I fully understood the situation, particularly as many interpreters have to be provided. When I pointed out that I needed no interpreter, we both had a good laugh. Hou saw that my case of forty-two years' absence from China was not the usual one and tried to see if something could be done for me. Three or four months later a message came calling me to the Liaison Office in Washington, D.C., to make the arrangement.

I chose the date of April 15, 1975, for my trip to Canton via Hong Kong. I wanted to attend the May First celebration in Peking. There are two good routes with direct flights to Peking, one from Paris and the other from Tokyo. But I decided to go to Canton via Hong Kong, for I wanted to see if I could bring some little gifts for my youngsters from there. Fortunately the China Travel Service Company in Hong Kong gave me a list of things I could take with me and offered to help transport them to their destination for me. So I stayed in Hong Kong for three days to make the arrangements before I caught the train crossing the border.

Though I had taken a good many long flights during the past thirty-odd years, I had never before felt my mind so blank as when setting out on this journey. I could not analyze what I was feeling—much joy as well as much sorrow were awaiting me. Many of my old friends tried to entertain me and to cheer me up with many comforting words. I could not find much to say, but tried hard to smile in reply. I told myself that I had had much bitterness and sweetness in my life already, yet I still could not imagine what sorts of emotions I was about to experience. Each life has its own joys and griefs. How many people could have tasted the strange emotions that filled me as I sat in the train bound for Canton—after having waited eight months for a visa? Lost in these thoughts, I seemed to reach my destination quickly and passed through the Chinese customs.

Not long afterward I was lying on my bed on the eighth floor of the Overseas Chinese Hotel. Before taking the elevator to go down for dinner, I gazed through my window at the ever-flowing waters of the famous Pearl River (or West River) which I had known some fifty years ago. It was the same muddy color as the Hudson River in New York, but here the river bed was much wider and a few Chinese-type boats were being towed by a small steamer. I exclaimed to myself that this was the old Canton all right, except for a steel-arched bridge, which I was told was newly constructed to take the place of one destroyed during the fighting. A big skyscraper, though not as high as many New York skyscrapers, a modern hotel that faced mine, accommodated mostly Western visitors. A lower building beside the skyscraper had been used as an exhibition hall for trade products during the twice-yearly Canton Fair to attract foreign buyers. As it proved to be too small for the show, a much bigger one had recently been constructed nearby for the exhibition.

I dined in the main hall with a big crowd of visitors, chiefly from Hong Kong and Southeast Asian countries. The noise was deafening, just like the old days I knew in Canton. I should probably be correct in saying that the Cantonese people tend to talk at a high pitch, louder than those of other parts of China. There were two more dining halls, each of which was full of similar noise. After forty-two years of comparatively quiet surroundings in European and American public eating places I felt this high-pitched talking rather hard to bear. Yet it had some attraction for my ear; this was south China after all. As the ground floor was not so quiet, I went up to my room and lay down on the bed imagining what to expect the next day in Peking. The many thoughts that filled my head helped me to sleep soundly that night.

V

In Peking and North China

DIRECTLY AFTER BREAKFAST, Hsieh Kung-li and Sung Wei-wen, both representatives of the China Travel Service, Canton branch, called on me and gave me an air ticket for Peking that afternoon. As the flight would not depart until four o'clock, Hsieh and Sung suggested showing me a bit of Canton. They knew I had been here some fifty years ago. But I had to admit that I could not remember anything of those remote days except the Pearl River. They agreed that Canton had changed much since the 1920s. We three had a short stroll along the riverbank and then went to see the trade exhibition in the new hall, which had been officially opened the previous day. In this big modern hall there were masses of products of every description beautifully arranged in their respective sections. A number of guides, chiefly young girls, explained the exhibits in English and other languages. Before I left China all manufactured articles, down to matches and sewing needles, were imported from Western countries or Japan. What a change to see them now with my own eyes, all manufactured by my fellow countrymen—an indescribable joy. I could also see the reason why a small black-and-white TV set, made in the United States, which a friend had asked me to bring over for his relative in Canton, was not allowed in. China now manufactures TV sets, cameras, wristwatches, motorcars, and even tractors herself. I was astonished to see them all in the exhibition as well as the many buyers from other lands, most of them apparently from Southeast Asia, Eastern Europe, and Africa. This means that China now need not spend money to import goods as in the old days, but earns foreign currency instead.

As I was no buyer, we only stayed for a brief survey, then went to see Dr. Sun Yat-sen's Memorial Hall commemorating the work of the founder of the Chinese Republic whom I had admired from my boyhood. We also had a look at the famous five-storied building, *Cheng-hai-lou,* or "Guarding-the-Sea Pavilion," built in the sixteenth century (Ming dynasty) when the south China coast had been greatly troubled by Japanese pirates. This pavilion is now used as a museum showing the history of Chinese ceramics, with the porcelains manufactured during the Han, T'ang, Sung, Yüan, Ming, and Ch'ing periods on different floors. I was particularly interested in seeing many fine pieces from the Shin-Wan kilns, which are situated near Canton—a famous local product. Another interesting building was the Sino-Russian Friendship Memorial Hall, built in the days when

Riding to work in the morning mist.

Stalin had sent his envoy Borodin to co-operate with the Chinese in Dr. Sun Yat-sen's new policy. Though this hall is well kept for the benefit of its many visitors, Dr. Sun, Stalin, and Mikhail Borodin were all dead and there appeared to be no other traces of Russian co-operation in Canton.

I was seen off by both Hsieh and Sung in the afternoon. The flight took about two hours and, on arrival at Peking airport, it was completely dark. As I walked toward the entrance of the airport building, the sound of "Father, Father" in Chinese came to my ears from not far away. There was nothing I could recognize in the voice, yet I had the impression that two or three people were calling in my direction. My heart began to thump and my whole being became agitated when I came face to face with the group who had come to welcome me—my friend, Hou Tung, who was briefly on leave from New York and his wife Ching Chao; Dr. T. T. Li, professor of foreign affairs at the Peking Institute of Foreign Relations; and of course my two daughters, two sons-in-law, and three grandchildren. Two of the young boys were my younger daughter's sons and the third boy was my elder daughter's. My elder daughter had come with her husband from Nan-ch'ang in our home province of Kiangsi, some 2,281 miles away from Peking, especially to welcome me. My eyes grew wet with joy and indescribable emotion at the sight of these youngsters. What were their feelings at that time, I wondered?

My second son-in-law, Liu Nai-tsung, born in Peking, is working as dramatic editor for a theater magazine, while his wife, Chien-lan, my younger daughter, now forty-five, teaches in a middle school at Di-an-men, or "Earthly Peace Gate," opposite the Tien-an-men, or Heavenly Peace Gate. She is also a barefoot doctor, going round the countryside to treat people with acupuncture. Their elder son, Tsung-wu, is at middle school and the younger one, Tsung-chun, at primary school. My elder son-in-law, Tan Chu-sheng, who majored in geology at his university and his wife, Hsiao-yen, my elder daughter, are both teachers in Nan-ch'ang; they have five children—four girls and one boy—but could only take the young son, Ding-ding, to Peking with them, for the four girls were all at school. When I learned that my two daughters and their husbands had all been given two months' leave with pay to accompany me, I was amazed at the generosity of the school authorities. I have never heard of such leniency in England and America. Naturally nothing made me happier than to have them show me around Peking, which I did not know well. The three young grandsons could hardly express their joy and attachment to me and were smiling all the time.

In my young days in China, no one could leave home easily, for lack of travel money. Now the authorities provide money for them, which is why many young students can travel to different parts of China and learn much more about their country. It was soon explained to me that many young students finishing their middle school studies would be sent to gain practical experience in a farming commune or factory. They might be sent at their own choice far away from home, but they would have one month's leave every year with pay and travel expenses to return home. Again, if the young graduate from middle school were an

A street scene in Peking.

only son or daughter, he or she would not be sent away from the parents, but would go to a nearby commune or factory. There was also a reasonable arrangement that if a family had two children graduating from middle school at the same time, only one would be sent away from home; the other would be given work in the same district. This was quite different from what I had heard about China in New York—that youngsters were forced to leave their homes and families against their will. My three young grandsons told me that they were waiting to be sent to some far-distant places after their graduation.

As my younger daughter had her house full with other relatives, including my elder daughter and family, I thought it would be simpler for me to take a room in the Hua-chiao-ta-hsia, or Overseas Chinese Hotel. As soon as my luggage was disposed of, I took my little family, eight of us, down to dinner. For the past forty-two years I had dined with many different kinds of people, but how strange I felt this time to be with my own daughters, their husbands, and my three grandsons. Never had I bothered about my age before, now I could not help realizing that I was of a different generation. This was the first time that we had all sat down face to face; I hardly knew how to start talking. Two of the young boys, smiling happily, gave me the menu for ordering dishes and helped me with good suggestions. Soon we all began to joke and chatter together. I enjoyed watching the three youngsters eating so well, yet not too greedily. I felt that I was really a happy grandfather.

After dinner, my younger daughter produced some rice coupons at the counter. She explained to me that only rice and cotton cloth were still rationed, for the output of these two commodities could not yet meet the enormous requirements of eight hundred million people. But the monthly ration of each was more than enough. I, as a visitor from abroad, did not need to produce any coupons. Nevertheless, this reminded me of those food-rationing days in England during World War II. Though food was short, the English government distributed it quite fairly all over the British Isles. But China covers an incomparably bigger area than Britain and has so many more people to feed; I could not help finding the rationing system admirably carried out, without fuss. Indeed, the Chinese mentality and nature have changed too, apart from the external changes I could easily see. That China, with its immense distances and enormous population, had been able to work out a fair rationing system in only twenty-five years was a miracle to me. Before the seven left me in the hotel that night, the three young grandsons reminded me not to forget the kind invitation from Uncle and Aunt Hou Tung to dine at the ancient and famous Peking Roast-Duck Restaurant the coming evening.

The next morning after breakfast, four of my old friends, whom I had known well in China before 1933, came to the hotel to see me. It was a great surprise to see them all together. They were all of my generation. As soon as we met, they heaved a satisfied sigh. "We have had peace for the past twenty-five years," they said. "No need to escape from place to place as we did before. No more war now—we've finished with it." One of them asked if I could still remember those days in the 1920s when we were fleeing hither and thither. Another told me that they had no inflation and all the daily commodities had had stable prices for more than twenty years. They all had work to do and were quite content with their lives now. I just listened without being able to add a word. I thanked them for their call and promised to see them again and again.

The author's younger daughter applying an acupuncture needle to a patient in Peking.

Presently Mr. and Mrs. Hou Tung came with my seven young ones to take me
out sight-seeing. With them was Yang Shu-tien from the head office of the China
Travel Service, who was to help with my travel arrangements as well as in locat-
ing my friends. There were a thousand and one places I wanted to see, but which
one should we go to first? The decision was the Summer Palace, better known in
Chinese as Yi-ho-yüan, situated to the northwest of Peking some eleven miles
away. Yang Shu-tien got hold of a sizable bus to take us there.

This palace was built by the Manchu empress dowager, Tzu-hsi, the ruiner of
China, who had squandered for her own pleasure the twenty-four million taels of
silver (one silver tael was worth more than ten U.S. dollars at the end of the nineteenth century) which had been collected and set aside for the government to
build a modern Chinese navy. Previously there had been a huge summer palace
in foreign style called Yüan-ming-yüan. It had been built in 1737 by the Manchu
emperor, Chien-lung, to the design of an Italian court painter of the time, Father J.
Castiglione, with the help of another artist, Father Beneist. These buildings had
been bombarded by the guns of the British and French in the war of 1860. Some
of the ruins still remain to remind the Chinese younger generation of what the
Western powers did to China in the past. The second summer palace which we
were going to see also suffered much damage in the sack of Peking in 1900 by
the eight allied Western powers, of which the United States was one. It had been

Morning health exercises in Peking Park.

Marco Polo Bridge outside Peking.

largely restored, repaired, and redecorated since the People's Republic of China was set up twenty-five years ago.

When we got out of our bus, there was already a big crowd moving through the main east gate, and we joined them. From the ancient Palace Hall we came to the Double Theater Pavilion where the former rulers, with their kin and courtiers, used to watch Peking Opera performances. A number of the pavilions were now used as exhibition rooms to display the gorgeous possessions of the last empress dowager: jade, enamels, and ceramics. It would have taken much time to examine and appreciate each exhibit carefully. I could not linger, but moved on with the rest to a long, open, covered walkway with its painted pillars and colorful ceiling decorated with romantic figures from the stories of the Three Kingdoms. Most Chinese, old and young, are familiar with these stories. My young grandsons tried hard to identify the heroes and events. This long passageway had been built along one bank of the K'un-ming Lake. We sat down for a while to watch the many small boats dotted over the lake, like giant water insects with red wings crawling over the water surface.

Formerly only members of the royal family, courtiers, and high officials had the privilege, shared by hundreds of court girls and many eunuchs, of walking around the palace grounds. From the T'ang dynasty, if not earlier, many hundreds of young, unmarried girls between thirteen and sixteen were brought to the palace by imperial decree every few years. Only a very few might have the chance to be seen by the emperor and spend a night or two with him. The majority remained unmarried till their deaths. With so many young, unmarried girls in the palace, no normal youths could be kept there; they had to be castrated to avoid unwanted children.

The late empress dowager, Tzu-hsi, was one of the girls summoned to the Manchu court. She was the daughter of a Manchu official. In her teens, though not very beautiful, she succeeded in getting herself chosen. After one or two years in the palace, when she still had not seen the face of the then reigning emperor, she showed her shrewd and wicked mind by bribing one of the eunuchs who used to carry the emperor about in a sedan chair within the enormous palace. Accordingly one evening the eunuch carried his royal master past her courtyard while she was playing a Chinese musical instrument—a bamboo pipe. The emperor was attracted by the music and asked to be carried inside the small court, where he and the music-playing girl spent the night together. She displayed all her charms and enough magic to entice the emperor to her court a few more times. Eventually the emperor entitled her *Fei-tzu,* a third-rank concubine. After that she became the emperor's lady and all the other girls were her servants. The eunuch who had brought the emperor to her became her favorite too. A few years later she was officially made the emperor's *huang'hou,* "second wife," for she had given birth to a son.

After the emperor died in old age, the first and second wives both became regents to this son of hers, the young emperor. As the first wife was a well-behaved and well-bred lady from a big Manchu family, with a quiet disposition and kind nature, she never had much to say during her regency. The second wife grasped all the power she could get and soon became a formidable person. Both regents were given the title *Huang-tai-hou* "empress mother" or "empress dowager," as Tzu-hsi was known in the West. After the death of the first empress mother, Tzu-hsi held the entire power over the young emperor. When he tried to accept advice for reform by changing the government into a parliamentary system headed by a monarch, like that of the English, Tzu-hsi squashed the idea and murdered the young emperor by poison. It was she too who encouraged the Boxer Uprising. The Boxers wanted to kill all the foreigners in China, thus inviting the eight Allied Western powers to take revenge and ransack the Peking palace.

As we sat by the lake, I was trying to visualize the former emperors, empresses, princes, and princesses with their retinues having been here to gaze at the scenery just like us; but they could not have seen so many laughing and smiling faces as we did nor could they have heard so much happy chatter. No outsiders were allowed into this Summer Palace in those days, so the life of those former palace girls could not have been enviable. This beautiful place was now for all to enjoy. We walked on to look at a small arbor with a curved roof called Chih-chun-ting, where I composed the following verse:

昆明湖畔知春亭
多少宮娥血淚痕
萬衆而今同笑語
游船紅星點點是

In the arbor of "knowing-the-spring" by K'un-ming lake,
How many blood-and-tear traces left by the palace girls!
Now hundreds and thousands of people laugh together,
The boats, one after another, are like red stars.

The former rulers had never imagined that this palace would cease to be enjoyed by their descendants. And the elaborate work formerly done by forced labor is now preserved for the pleasure of all who labor.

After some more wandering, we returned to our bus which took us to have a look at the Liu-li-ta, or "porcelain-tiled pagoda" on the Yü-chüan-shan, or "Jade Spring Mountain," one of the well-known landmarks in Peking. We also saw the enormous recumbent Buddha in Wo-fu-Sze; it is said to have been cast from fifty thousand pieces of copper by the Mongol emperor Kotpula with seven thousand workmen toiling on the project for ten years, from 1321 to 1331. It was still lying there and brilliantly polished, amazing after nearly five hundred years. I was also interested in the twelve small Buddhisativa figures—the twelve disciples of Buddha standing by while Buddha was about to enter Nirvana. They reminded me of the twelve apostles with Christ at the last supper. The number thirteen from then on became a bad omen in Christian countries. Buddha also had twelve disciples around his deathbed, making a group of thirteen, but this had no significance for Buddhists. How arbitrary superstitions are.

Afterward we found our way back to the city for a meal at the famous Peking Roast-Duck Restaurant, which was several hundred years old. I thought of the many Chinese restaurants in London, Paris, and New York. For many years I had eaten roast ducks said to be in the Peking style. They certainly could not compare with this centuries-old restaurant. I chuckled to myself when I remembered being told that many ducks from Long Island, New York, have been flown to Hong Kong and many other Southeast Asian countries. I think two of them could not equal one Peking duck, for these are specially fed and often called *tien-ya,* or "sweetened ducks"—fatter and ten-

Peking ducks in a big pond near Lishan.

derer than elsewhere. The most famous dish at this restaurant was the duck skins, beautifully roasted and crisp. Chinese have come here for centuries to eat the beautiful crispy skins. All the rest of the duck was cunningly used in the other dishes, so the whole dinner became a duck banquet, a sumptuous meal such as I had not eaten for years.

For my three young grandsons it might have been their first Peking duck. They ate their share with delight but they did not seem to understand why the roast duck should have been so sought after by their elders; to them many other dishes they had liked to eat before were just as good. I told them that though I did not know when the Chinese started to eat roasted ducks' skins, I had heard an amusing story about it in America. When the first Chinese envoy, Li Hung-chang, went to Washington, D.C., to open the Chinese legation there, he gave a sumptuous Chinese dinner for diplomats from different countries. After a number of dishes which they all ate with great appetite, there came a dish of roasted ducks' skins, which Li Hung-chang explained were a great delicacy. All the diplomats from European and South American countries stared at the dish and wondered what could be so good to eat about skins; none of them had seen it before. However, following Li Hung-chang, they all picked up a piece or two, helped by the legation servants, and ate and enjoyed them. But the American secretary of state inquired, "Why do we only eat the skins and where is the duck's meat?" Li Hung-chang began to say in a low voice, "The meat is for all your servants." My three grandsons

How Peking roast ducks are done in Peking.

burst out laughing. I then added that foreigners in the West called us Chinese "inscrutable"; they could not understand, for instance, why we loved to eat the duck's skin instead of the duck's meat.

To see the Great Wall of China was our next object. The same eleven of us, with two more—Hou's daughter and granddaughter—were driven west out of the city. Our destination was Pa-ta-ling, just beyond the famous Chü-yung-kuan, a wide gate or pass into the Wall. It was high up, over a thousand feet above sea level. This well-preserved part of the Great Wall, with plenty of space beside it for cars and buses to park, was visited evidently all the time. It was still early spring in these northern parts, neither cold nor warm, with the sun lighting up the whole scene as far as we could see. A good many people had already been climbing the wall. We chased after our four young children, who always liked to run and run until they had no breath left. There were several watchtowers in sight, the two highest ones topping two hills about two-thirds of a mile apart. Our youngsters still ran on ahead of us climbing toward the highest watchtower on our right. My friend looked at me as if asking whether I could manage to get up so far, considering my age of seventy-two. I smiled and just walked steadily on. We soon had all assembled there for the grandest view imaginable; it commanded the whole panorama of Chinese history since the third century B.C. when the building of the Great Wall started.

We walked slowly down again, but in a moment our four youngsters had disappeared and were next seen rushing up to another watchtower directly opposite us. We all followed after them again, but some of our group kept turning their heads to look at me inquiringly. I made no sign of weariness but also kept on with a smile. Again we reached the second summit, and another grand view, over an immense area that seemed to stretch onward without end. This Great Wall is a symbol for how much the collective effort of thousands of men working together can achieve. Each of us must contribute our personal energy to build another great wall to protect China.

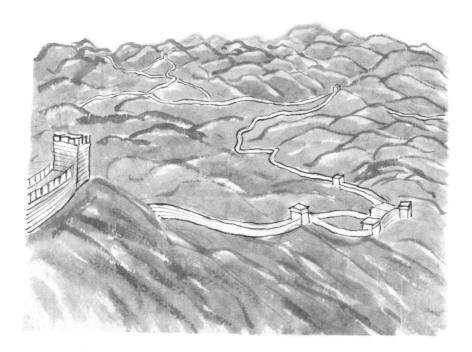

The Great Wall crawling among mountain ranges.

We had lunch boxes with us; so we sat down on the ramparts to rest and eat. Afterward we moved on from Pa-ta-ling to see the thirteen Ming emperors' tombs. They lie a little more than thirty miles from the gates of Peking and are considered to be one of the most interesting sights in the vicinity of the capital. On the way I saw the vast water surface of the Ming Tombs Reservoir which was built in 1958. The work force was led by the late Chairman Mao Tse-tung himself as one of the laborers. This reservoir has since altered the face of this arid area, turning it into a green valley.

The first emperor of the Ming dynasty, Chu Yüan-chang, set up his capital in Nanking and was later buried there. But his younger son, Yung-lo

Climbing up the Great Wall near Peking.

enthroned himself in Peking as the third emperor of Ming. In 1409 he started the construction of the first Ming tomb; subsequently twelve other Ming emperors and their empresses were buried together in this area. Emperor Yung-lo was a great statesman who sent one of his most able eunuchs, Cheng Ho, to lead a fleet of Chinese junks on a voyage through the South China Sea to what is now Malaysia.

We reached the tombs in less than half an hour. After passing the Great Red Gate we came to the Tablet House; from there we walked along the royal road, lined with great stone figures of attendants and elephants, camels, tigers, horses, and large imaginary animals. This led to the group of emperor's tombs arranged in a vast semicircle with the biggest tomb of Yung-lo in the center. Only one of the thirteen tombs had been excavated and that was Ting Ling, the tomb of Emperor Wan Li, the thirteenth emperor who ruled forty-seven years (1573–1620). The underground buildings of this tomb consist of three successive halls; the one in the middle has doorways on both sides leading to the annexes. There are altogether five connected chambers, grandiose in conception, making up the Underground Palace. Most of the treasures had been taken out and some were displayed in a special building nearby. We saw the golden crown of the emperor and two small, colorful crowns studded with precious stones and with pearl tassels for his two empresses. Many other priceless jewels for the ladies as well as many fine pieces of porcelain of the period demonstrated the beautiful workmanship of Chinese craftsmen in those feudal times. That kind of workmanship is still much encouraged but it is now for the enjoyment of all, not for individual royalty any more.

The second day in Peking had been very full and I slept soundly till late the next morning. Among the list of places I particularly wanted to visit was Yunkang in Shansi Province where the ancient Buddhist grotto carvings were to be found. When the late President Georges Pompidou of France was invited to China for a visit in 1973 he made a special request to see these cave grottoes; at that time they were still under restoration and repair. My request was approved too. As my friend Hou had soon to fly to New York for the United Nations General Assembly, he suggested accompanying me there for a few days, for he had never seen Yunkang either. I could not very well take my daughters and their husbands and children there with me, as this was a rather specialized visit. So Yang Shu-tien arranged berths for the three of us on the train to Tatung, capital of Shansi Province. After a rest and something to eat in the Shansi Hotel, we were driven, with Yang Chien-chang of the

A mule cart outside of Tatung, Shansi.

local authority and the representatives of the Shansi branch of China Travel Service, to the Yunkang caves.

In front of the main entrance stood Wu Chin-teh and Li Chin-yuan, both of the Office for the Protection of the Caves, ready to take us all round, outside and inside. There are a good many grottoes, some quite big and some small

A beautiful stone carving in the Yunkang caves, from about the beginning of the fifth century.

ones too, all filled with carvings. The first five were carved, I was told, between 450 and 455 A.D. and the rest were completed before the end of the fifth century. In the presently existing fifty-three caves there are more than fifty-one thousand statues of Buddha and Buddhisativas. All the caves are in the side of an enormous limestone hill which is about a mile long. As the caves had been dug out and carved some fifteen hundred years ago, there was naturally some erosion on the statues and some had been broken or damaged by chance robbers, as well as by Western archaeologists and officials who had tried to take some away for their museums. (As far as I can remember, there are three good pieces of the Yunkang carvings in the Metropolitan Museum of Art in New York and two others in Paris museums.) The carvings are certainly well-known to Western scholars and art collectors, who have written about them in their publications.

Apart from the few early animal carvings in stone, China has never created any enormous rock or stone sculptures like the Egyptians and Greeks. Though China's civilization is one of the oldest, she did not make much use of huge stones and rocks for buildings, as did the Egyptians and Greeks. However, when the Topo, a powerful chief from the northwestern region of China close to India, conquered the northern part of China and set up a dynasty there called Wei, he started to copy India in having great grottoes made for Buddhist temples. He was a devoted Buddhist and wanted to propagate the religion among the people he conquered and governed. Topo himself must have been in India and seen many famous grotto temples. When he decided to create similar grottoes in north China, no doubt he must have gotten some Indian designs to be used by local workers and artists in north China.

Among Western art forms stone or rock sculpture is as important, as architecture and painting. But we Chinese generally speak of calligraphy and painting and leave out sculpture and architecture. The point is that very little ancient architecture has survived intact, for the early Chinese buildings were built chiefly of earth and wood, which are perishable materials. Besides, the best Chinese buildings of the past were not associated with religious worship like the Christian cathedrals and churches. And our art historians have provided little historical account of our ancient architecture or examples of each period for study. Some modern students of architecture have been trying to work out some differences to be found in the wooden joints, the style of wood carvings, and so forth.

The earliest Chinese stone-carved horses still in existence date back to the third century B.C., while the large stone sculptures of the earliest Egyptian dynasties date back some five millennia. The Chinese art of rock sculpture came at a much later date—that is, Buddhist sculptures beginning from the middle of the fifth century A.D. The Yunkang grotto carvings provide the earliest examples of Chinese Buddhist sculpture. I must add that before 1933, when I was in China, no Chinese could have dreamed of seeing the Yunkang caves, for the site was unapproachable with no good roads, and with highwaymen and robbers on the route.

As the earth of Shansi Province is rich in coal, we also went to have a look round at the Yunkang coal mining company. I was surprised to see a number

Two young miners at the Yunkang coal mine, Shansi.

of youngish men, about twenty or under, working as coal miners and we exchanged greetings as they went down the mine. Quite a few young women were working on switchboards in one center or another. I was told that the output was more than triple what it used to be.

Sian, capital of Shensi Province, was our next stop—an ancient city some five hundred or more miles away from Tatung. This is a most respected ancient city, known as Changan since the third century B.C., when a Chinese civiliza-

A porcelain dragon door-guard of an ancient monastery at Tatung, dating from the ninth century.

tion began to put its roots down firmly. It was the capital first in the Han dynasty and then again in the T'ang dynasty. The T'ang period has usually been regarded by historians as China's golden age, for her literature, art, and military achievements and for the opening of the Silk Road to Rome over which trade and traffic passed to and fro, chiefly from Central Asia. Changan was then a great cosmopolitan capital with many Arabs, Turks and even Greeks and Romans living there.

After having settled in the Sian Hotel, we were taken to the highest part of the Ta-yen-ta, or the "Great Wild-Geese Pagoda," which was built in 646 A.D.

for the famous Chinese Buddhist monk, Hsuang-tsang who left China in 627, reached India in 633, and returned home in 645. He spent twelve years learning Sanskrit in India and brought back thousands of volumes of original Buddhist scriptures in Sanskrit which he later translated into Chinese almost singlehandedly in a monastery specially built for him. Ta-yen-ta was part of this monastery.

Afterward Yu Wen-ping, representative of the local branch of the China Travel Service, suggested that we should have a look at the City Museum. It houses a large number of excellent exhibits of T'ang objects from recent local excavations. I was particularly struck by the famous stone bas-relief of the horses which the T'ang emperor Tai-tsung used in his lifetime. There were six of those famous horses, but only four were on view in Sian; the other two had long ago traveled to the Philadelphia Art Museum.

Ta-yen pagoda in Sian Shansi.

Not far from the City Museum we were shown a recently excavated Neolithic site, some six thousand years old. The site is called Pan P'o and belonged to the Yangshao culture. It represents a remarkable example of the remains of a prehistoric tribal-communal settlement. The remains of a few house foundations, either quadrangular or circular, are preserved for visitors to see. We were told that a large quantity of bone instruments and farming tools, together with much pottery, rich in variety of decoration, some with painted designs, had been discovered in one of the remaining kilns. A preliminary study of the Pan P'o skeletons showed that they bore a close resemblance to the southern Asian Mongolians. The richness of these finds is indeed unprecedented and many archaeologists have been studying them carefully. There is little doubt that the people of Pan P'o must have played a significant role in the development of the early cultures of China.

While in Sian, it was a matter of course for us to go to Lin-t'ung, a few miles away, where the famous hot spring, Hua-ching-chih, is situated. Most Chinese have heard of this Hua-ching-chih, for it was where the T'ang emperor, Ming-huang took his favorite lady, Yang Kuei-fei to bathe. Many famous poems have been written about it and paintings have been made too. Yang Kuei-fei was considered the most beautiful woman in Chinese history and her plump, roundish face created a fashion at the time, as we can identify from paintings and figurines produced then. She was not only known to most Chinese, but also admired by the Japanese too. When I was visiting Kyoto I heard of a wooden statue, supposed to be a good and genuine representation of her, put high up in a small shrine in the Temple of the Bubbling Spring. I went to have a look at it, but it was very hard to see. A leaflet with the following description was distributed from the temple: "The Yang Kuei-fei kwannon, enshrined in this temple, is a lifelike statue of Yang Kuei-fei commissioned by the emperor of T'ang dynasty in China. It was brought here in 1255 by Tankei. The figure is celebrated as one of the most beautiful pieces of Buddhist sculpture in Japan." Just imagine she was worshipped in Japan as Kwannon, the Chinese Kuan Yin, or Goddess of Mercy. Not only that, there is a legend that this notorious beauty of China, who ruined the emperor Ming-huang, actually died in Japan. In 1969 my curiosity drove me to try to locate her supposed tomb in the Yamaguchi Prefecture. A local writer, Sukanari Miyazaki, was there to show me the spot and we discussed the matter at length, but he could not find a clear clue about how Yang Kuei-fei died in Kuzu in Yamaguchi. I told him that Chinese histories definitely say that Yang Kuei-fei died at Ma-wei P'o by strangling in A.D. 756 (see my book *The Silent Traveller in Japan*). How strange that she became a goddess in the country of our close neighbors.

After each of us had had a bath in the hot spring and before returning to the Sian Hotel, it was suggested that we visit the newly excavated tomb of Princess Yung-tai, a grandniece of the only woman emperor of China, Wu Tsai-tien, wife of T'ang Kao-tsung. This interested me much, for I already possessed a copy of the book containing the well-reproduced fresco paintings from that site. We entered the main gate and walked throught a long, whitewashed corridor to the inner chamber where the big stone coffin stood in the center. The original fresco had been taken away and preserved as a national treasure, but there was a copy of it along the whitewashed wall of the corridor on one side and on the other side was a series of recesses to house a good many small pottery figurines, horses and

A drawing from the old T'ang fresco inside Princess Yung-tai's tomb.

riders on horses, such as one can see in Western museums. Outside of this royal tomb there were two long rows of stone-carved figures and animals lined up on both sides like those in front of the Ming tombs in Peking. We walked around to look at a number of them. Then we came to a squarish stone with a deep bas-relief of a bird that looked like an ostrich, which surprised me greatly. How could an African ostrich be known to a Chinese stone carver in the seventh century? This also indicated to me that the stone carver had some freedom of choice in the subjects he wanted to carve; he was not limited to the stone figures of civil and military officials with the usual elephants, camels, lions, and horses.

We had left the Sian Hotel on a sunny morning but came back under a cloudy sky. Originally we had planned to fly to Yenan for a brief visit, but we were told that with the weather being uncertain, we might not then be able to get back to Peking for the May First celebration. As my friend Hou had to fly to New York for the General Assembly on May 2, we decided to leave Yenan for my next visit and went to Hu-hsien for a day before we returned to Peking.

Hu-hsien is one of the many counties in Shensi Province, but it has lately become well-known throughout China for having many good peasant-artists working in its communes. This was an unheard of thing in the past—a peasant who could paint—for in the old days, few of them could have any education, let

A T'ang stone bas-relief of an ostrich.

alone be taught to handle a brush. I naturally wanted to meet them and to talk about their work. Most of the local artists and the educational body welcomed us with smiling faces. We were shown round two exhibition rooms containing their works. Most of them represented countryside activities and life in the communes, all in realistic images. I readily acknowledged their merit, for they possessed the gift of rendering their subject matter explicitly with artistic arrangement. Two or three pieces could be compared with "Women in the Field Working" by the French artist, Jean François Millet or Vincent van Gogh's "Potato Eaters." I had a good talk with Liu Chih-teh, whose painting of an old peasant-fighter before liberation sitting peacefully and reading a work of Chairman Mao has been reproduced in color over and over again and in many different sizes. The work was so very different from the traditional type, for it showed the subject in three dimensions and the facial rendering with light and shade. In the Chinese traditional type of painting human figures were not always good in proportion, for the artists never studied anatomy. I told Liu that his work, apart from its artistic value, could help many who saw it to understand the deeper significance of the subject.

Mealtime in a commune outside Peking.

That these peasants could paint so well was a surprise to me. Many Westerners with their knowledge of modern art in the West have criticized present-day China for having neglected it. But they do not realize that the real function of art in China in the past twenty-five years has been to educate through pictures, good pictures too, rather than by teaching in words. Liu Chih-teh told me that he had been a peasant since his childhood and did not have enough chance to study before. He had always from his youth been interested in pictures and now, as the secretary of the local Revolutionary Committee for years, he had found time to paint at odd moments. I told him that I envied him having so many models at hand for painting anytime he fancied. I lived in New York and life there was very hectic with little time to do painting let alone find models. He laughed. I encouraged him to sketch much and as quickly as he could, for each quick sketch might have caught a movement which he had never imagined before. Our discussion was only interrupted when a young peasant-girl artist came to join us. Her jovial, smiling face drove away all seriousness. Her name was Liu Fang and she had painted a sensitive representation of the village life she knew so well. How much has changed in China during the past twenty-five years.

A mule cart in north China.

May First is the important festival of labor celebrated annually. The other important Chinese festival is October First, the National Independence Day. China has now become independent completely and absolutely, which is a joy for any China-born Chinese like me whenever I think of it. Most visitors would like to be in Peking to attend one or the other of these two festivals, for each is a well-organized celebration with many displays and performances. On May First, nearly all the inhabitants of the city were out, mingling with various groups or strolling in the streets, particularly in the Tien-an-men Square which could easily hold over a hundred thousand people without much crowding. Hou was busy packing and calling on friends before flying to New York, so he could not go round with me. My youngsters had their own arrangements for the celebration day. Yang Shu-tien gave me a special ticket for the displays and entertainment area at Yi-ho-yuan.

Everywhere were colorful hangings on the trees and around the platforms. There were dancing, orchestras, singing solo or in groups, acrobats, and traditional *wu-shu,* or "national wrestling exercises"—about twenty different sections and Yang Shu-tien and I stopped at quite a number for a short while. The sun was shining brilliantly, lighting up the whole of Peking, with its buildings old and new, its trees and parks, while masses of national flags in vermilion red were waving and shimmering in the air, brighter than ever in the clear sunlight. Gaiety and merrymaking filled every corner. In my younger days I used to be taken out to see our Lantern Festival in the city streets, which were crammed with spectators on those occasions. But often some unpleasant incidents took place or we ran into pickpockets. When I grew older the Lantern Festival was banned because of wars or civil strife. In the past fifty years or so I have never seen so many people assembled and mingling together in such an orderly way without the slightest disturbance anywhere. I could not believe it and simply thought that the nature of all Chinese must have changed. I was told that nearly forty thousand people had participated in the display. This celebration was being held under authoritative control and those who had organized it so well had my greatest admiration.

Historically Peking is the very heart of China, dating back some seventeen hundred years, and each section of the land could have much to tell. I made the best of my two-week stay, seeing as many interesting places as possible, particularly with the help of my own youngsters, several of whom knew the city thoroughly. I visited the old Palace grounds, the Imperial Gardens, the Memorial to the People's Heroes, the National Museum of Natural History, the Museum of Arts and Crafts, and also the Museum of History with its exhibits of relics from ancient times.

I must make special mention of our visit to the Zoological Gardens to see that special animal of China, the Giant Panda. This rare animal must have been living on the high mountains of western China for centuries but it was only discovered

The May First Festival in Peking.

Three of my grandsons on a bronze lion door-guard outside Peking Palace.

by chance by a French Jesuit game hunter, Père David, in 1876, when he was overtaken by darkness on the slopes of those high mountains one evening and had to find shelter for the night. He entered a small hut where an old peasant and his wife were living. He noticed a rug on the ground made of black and white fur and asked what animal skin it was. The answer was, a local white bear occasionally seen on the mountainside. Père David examined the rug and began to make inquiries about the creature and to study it. In 1911 a Western game hunter shot one of these bears; it was eventually stuffed and sold to the Dublin Museum of Natural History. I saw it there while on a visit to Dublin in 1948. Soon the news of this rare animal went round the world and every big game hunter wanted to catch one alive. In the spring of 1938, an American game hunter, Lloyd Smith, caught five live ones—four fully grown and a baby of only four months— and brought them all to London. He sold the mature ones to European zoos and the baby to the London Zoological Society in Regents Park. With its two black ears, two black circles round the eyes, four black legs, and the rest of its head and body pure white, its pigeon-toed walk and merry antics, the rare little creature looked comic and appealing. The first day it was shown to the public it created a great sensation and excitement in London. Many came to see it from the Continent and the London Zoo was packed for months. Since I was living in London at the time and this creature came from my country, I naturally went with the crowd. At once it struck me that its black and white color scheme would be suitable for Chinese brush rendering. I decided to study it carefully and to sketch

Visitors to the Peking Zoo.

it in all poses for some Chinese-style paintings. As its stable diet is bamboo leaves and young stems, it is an ideal subject for a typical Chinese work.

Since this creature came from the high mountains of western China, about twelve thousand feet above sea level, where it was cool and seldom exposed to much sunlight, even the mild London sun would make it sleepy in the daytime. So being a fellow of the Zoological Society, I made a special arrangement with the late Dr. G. Vevers to sketch it at night. I got quite a number of rough sketches and started to work on them with Chinese ink and brush on the semiabsorbent Chinese paper. Many Chinese painters in the past had painted all kinds of beasts and birds, but not this creature, for it was not known to them. So I became known as the first Chinese painter to have painted the giant panda. I also wrote two children's books called *Chinpao and the Giant Pandas* and *The Story of Ming*. The former was translated into Japanese and the latter into Hindustani and Bengali. The London critics soon dubbed me the panda man.

When the new central government was set up in Peking in 1949, it declared that no giant pandas could be exported because of their rarity. After a good many years of experiment, giant pandas were bred in the Peking Zoo. Though still rare, their numbers have slowly increased and the zoo authority in Peking seemed assured that it would continue to breed. This enabled the Peking government to present, as a friendly gesture, a pair of giant pandas each to Moscow, Paris, London, Tokyo, Washington, D.C., and now a pair to Sydney, Australia. A Japa-

萬牲園裡大熊貓

Two giant pandas in the Peking Zoo.

nese friend of mine, Risabro Marukami had his translation of *Chinpao and the Giant Pandas* published in Japan in 1974 to meet the excitement there when Peking's present was shown in Tokyo.

With all these connections in the past, how could I resist going to see the inspirer of some of my work while I was in Peking? My daughters and their husbands and three young grandsons all went with me. The youngest grandson kept calling to me whenever one of the giant pandas showed an inclination to come out of its den.

Later, I went to see my old friend, Wu Tso-jen, president of the Chinese Academy of Art, who has been famous for his giant panda pictures since he started to paint them in the 1950s. Many of his paintings have been used for designs on Chinese stamps. How happy the giant pandas would be if they understood how they have helped us in our art. Mrs. Wu Shu-fang paints flowers and children.

I knew that a few buildings were still under repair or restoration and were not yet open to the public, so I asked if it would be possible to see the Temple of Heaven and the Altar of Heaven. The answer was affirmative. So I took seven of my youngsters with one more of their friends to accompany me. Yang Shu-tien had other things to attend to. The nine of us went by bigger car driven by Hsiao Chang, who had already driven me on other trips. We had a visit to Yi-ho-yuan again, but this time we had lunch in a garden up a small hill behind the Hsieh-ch'u-yuan, or "Harmonious enjoyment garden," which we had missed on our first visit. This is a much quieter quarter and known to be suitable for writing poetry and painting.

Then we went on to see the Temple of Heaven, some three miles away from the capital. The Temple of Heaven consists of three main buildings in a straight line; first, the Chi-nien-tien, then the Imperial Vault of Heaven, and third, the Circular Mound or Altar of Heaven. Originally the Chi-nien-tien served as the place for the former emperors to worship; only in later times did it become the

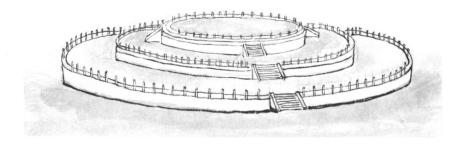

A general design of the Altar of Heaven in Peking. No great architecture without a roof is to be found anywhere else in the world.

Hall of Prayer for a good harvest. We started from the Chi-nien-tien, where in the old days the imperial head would lead a procession of ministers and a retinue to perform a ceremony; they then would proceed to the distant Altar of Heaven to pay homage to the Supreme Lord of Sublime Heaven, the ruler of the Universe. China, unlike other countries, never set up a system of religion, but instituted the worship of Heaven. Though this kind of superstitious worship has been dispelled by modern science—one can even fly to the moon—the grandeur of the master plan with its beautiful architectural achievement must still be admired. It is said that Yung-lo, the third emperor of the Ming dynasty, conceived and caused to be erected the three wonderful structures known as the Temple of Heaven.

In front of the entrance steps before we went up inside the Chi-nien-tien there were a good many people standing on a central piece of rock clapping their hands hard; I was told that one could hear an echo there. This was new to me, for usually an echo could be heard if one were enclosed by a thick wall, but not in the open. We all tried and my two grandsons said that they did hear the echo but I could not. The second building, the Imperial Vault of Heaven, or Huang-chiung-yu in Chinese, is a round building with a circular roof, no pillars inside, but with delicate openwork tracery and a wooden screen. The third is the Tien-tan, or Altar of Heaven, a monument consisting of three round layers, all in white marble, having no tiles, no roof, no doors, no windows—only steps leading from the lowest and widest to the middle and then to the upper platform. This altar can be best described in the words of an Englishman, Dr. S. Wells Williams, who wrote about it in the early 1920s:

> The altar is a beautiful triple circular terrace of white marble, whose base is 210, middle 150 and top 90 feet in width, each terrace encompassed by a richly carved balustrade. The uppermost terrace whose height above the ground is about eighteen feet, is paved with marble slabs, forming nine concentric circles—the innermost of nine stones including a central piece and around this each receding layer consisting of a multiple of nine until the square of nine is reached in the outer row. It is upon the single round stone in the center of the upper plateau that the emperor kneels when worshiping Heaven and his ancestors at the winter solstice.

Just imagine such a well-designed piece of architecture without a roof. Though the ancient Chinese had their reasons for such a structure, the Westerners who first saw it could not understand it. For myself, I think these three structures as a whole form the most beautiful construction I have ever seen in the whole world. I have traveled as widely as I could during the past forty-two years, but have found nothing like the Temple of Heaven anywhere. I admire the present government in Peking for having repaired and restored it to its original grandeur as one of the most strange but beautiful pieces of architecture that was ever designed by man.

Before I returned to China, rumors that most of the ancient buildings had been destroyed or torn down were widespread in Europe and America. The Temple of

Heaven with its ancient beauty should give the lie to all these baseless rumors. I think the three structures of the Temple of Heaven should be viewed from higher ground under clear moonlight when the color of the red walls, the glazed blue tiles, and the pure white marble blending together breathe an ethereal beauty impossible to describe. Perhaps a tall viewing tower should be built inside the cypress forest nearby.

There are far too many historic landmarks in Peking to be seen in a few days or even months. In my two weeks I could not spend every moment on such sight-seeing. Whenever I had some spare time I would travel out with my youngsters through the lanes and streets, join the queues to enter the smallest eating places possible, and enjoy watching the smiling faces and listening to their chatter. I never remember the old generation being such a cheerful lot. Once I stopped at the side of a street where a crowd of buyers were surrounding a big load of different vegetables such as carrots, cabbages, turnips, spring onions, spinach, and many others. All were packed on top of a rather small pushcart; it looked as if

A vegetable seller on a Peking street.

some would drop off at any moment. Though the people surrounding the cart were numerous, it seemed to me that they could not buy the whole lot. As soon as the seller had a moment I asked whether he would take the vegetables back home if he could not sell them all. No, he said, the rest would be left where they were. He assured me that no one would take any away without paying, even though he himself went home for the night. I was amazed that not even a small carrot would be stolen in the night.

Sometimes my youngsters would encourage me to jump on a bus which would take me to some place they wanted to show me. No sooner did I get on than someone would get up to let me have the seat. I thought they were all so sensitive about my age, but my second daughter joked about my Western collar and tie having an influence on people. We all had a laugh and our fellow passengers joined in. Though Peking had only three million fewer people than New York, its buses are neither so numerous nor so frequent. Whichever one I caught with my youngsters was always full to capacity. Though I enjoyed the courteous treat of having a seat given to me, I felt rather embarrassed at times. Even in a very crowded small eating place, I would not be left standing for long. It was fun and I quite felt myself one of the masses while I was exploring Peking. After four o'clock in the afternoon, nearly every big store, such as the East-Wind Market or the Hsin-hua Book Company, was crowded with customers so that there was hardly room for us to go through. This told me that the people now had money to spare for some extra food or clothing. They were also interested in reading. What a different attitude and situation now from what I knew of the masses before 1933.

Only one particular street, called Wang-fu-ching-ta-chieh, kept me in deep thought whenever I walked through it. This used to be called Morrison Street, so named after an Australian journalist, George Morrison, formerly a *London Times* correspondent. The northern war lord Yüan Shih-kai had sought support from him for his enthronement as the emperor of a new dynasty. Morrison must have been a strange foreigner. In his book *An Australian in China,* published in 1922, he wrote that he traveled "as a Chinese, dressed in warm Chinese winter clothing, with a pigtail attached to the inside of my hat"; and again, "I engaged three new men in Suifu, who undertook to take me to Chaotong, 230 miles, in 13 days, special inducement being held out to them in the shape of a reward of one shilling each to do the journey in eleven days. Their pay was to be 7 shillings and 3 pence each." Just imagine a reward of one shilling had to be held out as a special inducement. For only seven shillings and three pence each, three poor Chinese

A street scene in Peking.

coolies had to carry his heavy luggage for 230 miles in eleven days. No wonder so many Westerners wanted to live in China in those days. They could not live there so easily now.

While in the capital, I also made a special point of seeing a few light-industry factories—arts and crafts for which Peking has long been renowned in the past.

An enamel worker in a Peking factory.

Many good and noted craftsmen had died, because they had been unable to make a living while so much disturbance and civil war were going on. One of them, the noted craftsman, Yeh Feng-chi, whose special skill was in the painting of fine designs inside small glass snuff bottles, never more than two inches long, was known to me and I wanted to see him in person. In one factory we came to the snuff-bottle section, but unfortunately learned that Yeh had died only a month before. Before liberation he could not make a proper living from his art, for no-

An ivory engraver in a Peking factory.

A woman expert painting the inside of a glass snuff-bottle in a Peking factory.

body was using snuff, and there were no collectors to buy the bottles. After the establishment of the new government in Peking, he was particularly singled out and asked to work in the factory with pay, and also to train a number of young people in the nearly dead art technique. He did train ten or more people for a few years before he passed on. He had trained his own daughter from her youth and she is now working as the leader of the section. I watched her use a very fine hooklike brush to paint figures inside a glass snuff bottle, displaying most un-usual ability. The thin lines and minute dots could not be distinguished by human eyes. I asked why these snuff bottles were still being made if no people were using snuff nowadays. The answer was that many Westerners were still crazy about collecting them. I also saw a number of jade carvers in the factory who seemed to continue the traditional crafts without a break. One or two jade carvers were trying to work out new designs appropriate to the modern age, not strictly following the ancient subject matter. I thought this was an improvement, for our creative work should keep pace with the time we live in.

In another factory I went to see the work by a craftsman known as Ni-jen Chang who could knead clay into human figures or animals in the most intricate lifelike manner; he did human portraits as well. Many of his pieces had been shown in Europe and he was even invited to demonstrate his art in Paris. Another craftsman was Mien-jen Lang, who could work flour paste into groups of theatri-cal figures, chiefly illustrating stories from the book *The Romance of Three King-doms*. I watched him doing one of those figures in full dress. He told me that he was a happy man now for he could just work on the subject that interested him

An old jade carver in Peking.

with all the materials provided by the factory, unlike the old days when he hardly managed to sell enough for a proper meal, yet had to find money to get new materials.

Years ago I was taken to see the famous Gobelin factory in Paris, where they have manufactured the world-renowned tapestries since the fourteenth century. I walked around there slowly, carefully observing each process. Many of the workers followed the old system with traditional designs. Others, influenced by modern art movements in France such as cubism and abstractism, had created a new vogue for very bright and strong colors. Peking rugs and carpet weaving have been well-known, too, throughout the world. The simple and typically Chinese-painting-like designs have been preferred to the complicated and intertwining designs of Persian rugs and carpets. In a Peking carpet factory I found the technique quite similar to that for the Gobelin tapestries, though the designs were naturally different. I discussed with the person in charge of the factory whether some bright-colored designs could be used. His answer was, "Why not?" provided they would harmonize with the setting and other arrangements in the room or hall.

I next visited a needlework and embroidery factory. In this branch of Chinese craft, the Peking stitches are well-known but the products have to yield precedence to the *Hsiang-hsiu,* or "embroidery of Hunan," *Soo-hsiu,* or "embroidery of Soochow," and *Che-hsiu,* or "embroidery of Chekiang." These come first, second, and third in the line. Chinese embroidery has had a world reputation for centuries. In the factory I was shown a new invention called *liang-mien-hsiu,* a piece of embroidery in which the design appears equally clearly on both sides.

There were no rough places or messy ends anywhere. I examined a piece carefully from all directions but could not find the ends of the colored silks.

Peking also has heavy industries—the Peking steel factory, for instance. Visiting this factory one morning I found a number of workers pouring an enormous cauldron of liquid ore through regulated tunnels and tubes. I was standing with some others on a higher iron structure and could feel the intense heat when the molten iron was poured. To my great surprise two women workers in their boiler suits were close to the furnace. I have seldom seen women working in heavy industries in Western countries. Chinese women seemed a step ahead in equality from this point of view. Another thing that surprised me in that same factory was an exhibition of calligraphy by the workers. I went through it piece by piece with exclamations at quite a few. My mind went back immediately to the old days when I was in China and knew hardly any worker who could read or write. Workers then had to bribe the *kung-tou,* or "foreman" to give them work and were often cheated in their wages, for they simply did not know what was written on the wage slip. Now they could even produce artistic calligraphy. I could not believe my own eyes.

China has long been credited with the invention of printing. She is also known to have been the first to invent many-color printing by wood blocks in the seventeenth century. In those early days China only reproduced wood-block prints of flower-and-bird subjects. The method was then introduced to Japan where the Japanese printers used it for a much wider range of subjects—illustrations of the theater and actors as well as pictures of famous ladies, known as *Ukioe* work. In fact, they have so refined the technique that Japanese wood-block prints have

A street scene in Peking.

become a craft admired and collected throughout the world. The Japanese wood-block makers were themselves noted artists—Hokusai, for instance.

In recent years, dating from the early 1920s, Yung-pao-chai, a special stationery and printing firm in Peking, has reproduced many well-known Chinese ink paintings using a new technique for printing without any oil-based ink. The block is first made from the original work and then only the necessary water color is applied for printing. The result is so good that these reproductions are almost as lively as if the artist had actually painted them. However, unlike the normal printing with greased ink, only one impression can be made for each application of water color. So for each printing, the coloring must be repeated as before, by hand. Therefore the printer must be an artist as well, for he or she must know about the necessary gradations of the colors. Not being mass-produced, each print could bring more satisfaction to the buyer or collector. When I went through the actual printing section, I noticed the printers were all women and evidently artists. I watched carefully how one of them took up a brush, dipped it in the prepared water color, brushed it over the wood block which was held in the other hand, and then pressed it on Chinese semi-absorbent paper. A few minutes later she hung the printed result on the wall like a new painting just finished. This technique has been greatly improved since the old days and can be employed for very fine and intricate pieces of old Chinese painting.

While I was there, the director of the studio-factory took me to see the almost finished reproduction of a Sung painting entitled "Han Hsi-tai Entertaining Guests at Home in the Evening," an eleven-foot-long handscroll with more than sixty figures of men and women in many colors. About three thousand wood blocks of different sizes were made for the different colors. Using these three thousand small wood blocks each in turn, one can imagine how long it would take to finish the print. Each color registration must be exact; exquisite handling and great patience are required. The resulting handscroll differed only slightly from the original and the soft color surface of the entire work gives a far better effect than the shiny surface of a print made by modern machines. I think Yung-pao-chai has created a new type of colored wood-block printing and it will no doubt have a wider use in the future.

While still in Peking I managed to find time to see many of my good friends whom I had not met for nearly half a century, including my old professor Chang Tzu-kao, who had taught me inorganic chemistry and physical chemistry in 1922 and 1923. Now at the age of ninety-one, he still remembered me clearly. I also saw General Li Ming-yang who was the commander of the troops which I joined in 1926. Hsü Teh-heng, deputy chairman of the People's Congress Assembly, came from my native city and was a schoolmate of my elder brother. I had heard of him since my childhood but never met him, for he went to study in France when I was a young boy. I decided to pay him a call and was well received with a great happy smile. He was then over eighty years of age and talked about himself and my brother during their school days in Kiukiang. He asked about Kiukiang, our birthplace, when I was there before 1933, and assured me that I would see great changes when I went there next month.

From the beginning of the twentieth century Kiukiang has produced many men who devoted their lives to changing China into a better country for her people. Many joined the first revolution led by Dr. Sun Yat-sen, such as Chang Hua-fei who sacrificed his life at Huang-hua-kang in 1908. Another one, Huang Yuan-yung, a noted journalist, was assassinated by Yüan Shih-kai's men in San Francisco in 1915. Hsü Teh-heng and my brother both nourished revolutionary thoughts when they were schoolboys; Hsü then went to France to study and my brother joined Dr. Sun Yat-sen's movement in Canton in 1916. Hsü felt satisfied that he had followed Chairman Mao and had helped to establish the present government. He had struggled for his ideas and convictions for almost sixty years. I gave him a deep bow on leaving his house.

I also managed to see three of my university mates from fifty years ago. Dr. Wu Yu-shun, deputy president of China's Academy of Science, and Dr. Yen Chi-tzu, a noted physicist of the same Academy, both gave me a delicious lunch in a famous Peking restaurant. Dr. Li Shan-pang, a geologist specializing in earthquake science, came to my hotel and we talked about our old days for almost a whole day. Dr. Cheng Hsi-meng, an economist at the Council for Promoting International Trade, had dinner with me at my hotel and we remembered our happy moments together in London in 1934–35. Yeh Chun-chien took me to his home at Ti-an-men for a lunch specially prepared by Mrs. Yeh full of our native flavor; we all had come from the same area of China on the Yangtze River. Yeh has been the assistant editor of the English magazine, *Chinese Literature*, since 1950. I felt very happy and lucky to have met so many old friends while in Peking.

VI

Tachai to Chengchow

ANY STUDENT of Chinese history must have been wondering how the successive dynasties of China's past managed to keep the population well fed and cared for. Not much has been written on the subject in the history books as far as I have discovered. With the huge population China has always had, to feed them adequately should be the prime concern of any central government. The weak Manchu government of the past hundred years never tried to tackle this problem, which in fact became more acute in the last thirty years of their rule. When China became a Republic after the first success in driving out the Manchu royal house, the people did not get a better life, but their suffering was even more and worse

An old mule cart in north China.

with the rise of the war lords. Almost every summer, I used to see in China large groups of refugees from the north coming down to my city begging for food when the Yellow River flooded their lands or when famine occurred. In his book, *China, Land of Famine,* Walter H. Mallory, former secretary of the China International Famine Relief Commission, wrote in 1929:

> The food problem is an ancient one in China: from the earliest times famines have been an ever-recurring scourge. . . . Untold millions have died of starvation. . . .

The great drought that occurred in North China in 1920–21 during which, according to the best obtainable information, five hundred thousand of the natives perished, is still fresh in the minds of the public. Mr. Dwight W. Edwards, in his comprehensive report, estimates that at the height of the distress nearly twenty million people were destitute. In some of the worst affected districts not only was the entire reserve of food consumed but also all other vegetation. A house-to-house canvass revealed the following bills of fare: *k'ang*, mixed with wheat blades, flour made of ground leaves, Fuller's earth, flowerseed, poplar buds, corncobs, *hung ching tsai* (steamed balls of some wild herb), sawdust thistles, leaf dust, poisonous tree bean, *kaoliang* husks, cottonseed, elm bark, bean cakes (very unpalatable), peanut hulls, sweet potato vines ground (considered a great delicacy), roots, stone ground up into flour to piece out the ground leaves. Some of the food was so unpalatable that the children starved, refusing to eat it.*

I can confirm that the above words are absolutely correct, for in my young days I often heard my elders saying how people in the northern provinces like Shensi ate grasses and roots and any vegetation they could get hold of to relieve their hunger. Besides, in the countryside in those provinces, two or three people would sometimes have to share one ragged pair of trousers. Others would just cover themselves up somehow like prehistoric men. However, this time when I came to Peking, Tatung, Sian, and many other cities of north China, I did not see a single such pathetic individual. Everyone looked well fed and properly dressed.

Two young miners discussing their work in north China.

They joked with each other while working on their jobs happily. This is the important point that any visitors who may be students of Chinese history should take special note of when considering the differences from the old China.

Many people in government work or communes and factories informed me

* W. H. Mallory, *China, Land of Famine* (New York: American Geographical Society, 1928).

Modern terraced fields in Tachai, Shansi.

that the reconstruction of Chinese agriculture was listed as the first urgent task after the setting up of the central government in Peking in 1949. The famous production brigade of peasant-workers in the Tachai community in Shansi Province seemed to have been hard at work and to have had good results, though not without some terrible failures at first, in turning the absolutely barren wilderness of their area into a cultivable one with good crops growing. Their achievement was made known throughout the entire country with the saying of Chairman Mao, ''Agriculture should follow the example of the Tachai production brigade.'' Therefore, ''Nung yeh hsueh Tachai,'' 農业学大寨, or ''In agriculture learn from Tachai,'' written in big Chinese characters was posted everywhere on the walls and hillsides, as well as on many specially erected stands. No one could escape these five characters. Visitors from foreign countries regard them as extensive advertisements. Even if they cannot read Chinese, many become weary of those big Chinese characters just as they dislike their own big advertisements; but they do not understand that this is a way of teaching the Chinese masses to solve their food problems.

As Tachai has been so much in the public eye, many people from other provinces as well from some Western countries go to see Tachai to find out how the work goes on there. I was urged to go and went with Yang Shu-tien, staying there for two nights and three days. Li Yu-hsi from the Tachai production brigade met us with a car when we got out of the train. We were driven through miles of countryside with terraced fields backed by yellow and darkish-yellow hills in the distance. I had never been in this northern part of China before and was surprised to observe many holes and caves dug out of the hillsides which I was told had been the homes of the peasants and their families in the not too distant past. Very few lived in such hill-holes now. I was appalled to think of people living in those conditions, but Li admitted that he and his family had lived in a cave before 1949 and had regarded themselves as quite lucky, for some did not even have that shelter. Now the people worked together collectively to grow more and they produced more than enough for their own needs.

New housing at Tachai.

After lunch, a cheerful young woman, Chia Tseng-so, second in charge of the Tachai production brigade, came and talked to us. She gave us a general description of the work of remodeling the Tachai landscape, beginning in 1953 when she was only four years old. Tachai covers quite a large piece of land at the base of the well-known Hu-tou-shan, or Tiger-Head Hill, one thousand meters above the sea level. It is a part of the T'ai-hang mountain range, with its yellowish sandy soil, or loess, which was brought under cultivation earlier than any other region in China. When Chairman Mao and his army came to liberate the land, each peasant received a portion of land to work for himself. Under Chairman Mao's direction and straightforward policy they were taught to organize themselves to work together in co-operatives and then to form the co-operatives into communes.

Chia Tseng-so was born in the year when the Peking government was set up. But she studied well in her girlhood and, when she was twelve, joined the hard work of carrying stones and shoveling sand, cutting rocks and collecting soil.

Moving stones and rocks together for building a dam.

Through her understanding of government policy and plans she was later elected to be the deputy head of the Tachai Revolutionary Committee, which was in charge of all the affairs of the Tachai Commune.

I also went to see the Commune's medical rooms, with a resident doctor and two assistants. There were several beds for patients. The doctor took me to see his pharmacy where he had an assistant to manufacture pills for urgent needs. All this was new and interesting to me, for I knew that in the old days peasants in the countryside could not get to see doctors, but simply waited to die. This also reminded me of the Australian flying doctors who would fly to see the patient whenever he had a distant call, for Australia is so vast and it is not easy to get to a remote place except by air.

Later Chia Tseng-so and Li Yu-hsi came to take us to see two neighboring communes, a big tunnel in the making, and a large dam being built with about eight or nine hundred people working there. The prosperous wheat and corn growing in the fields made it difficult for me to imagine how the same land could have been so treacherous and caused such famine years ago. The earliest generations of peasants would have worked as willingly and hard as the present ones if the government then had had a policy and plan. I knew that most of the countryfolk during my term of office in three different counties would have wanted to work if I could have provided it for them; but nothing was organized. No one likes to be starving and to eat grasses and roots. The Tachai brigade gained their reputation by working hard collectively and willingly.

Boys and girls working together to transport earth for the construction of a big dam near Tachai, Shansi.

On the last evening I composed the following little verse:

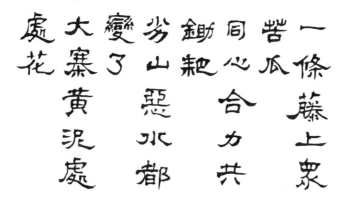

Like a long stem where hang many bitter melons,
With one heart and combined effort, they plough and harrow together!
The treacherous hills and wicked water are all transformed,
In the yellow soil of Tachai, blossoms everywhere.

We left Tachai in the morning to catch a train for Chengchow via Shih-chia-chuang, the capital of Hopeh Province. When the train reached Shih-chia-chuang, Wang Pao-fu, representing the local branch of the China Travel Service, met us and suggested that we should have a rest first, for the next train to Chengchow would not arrive for another three hours or so. After a few sips of Chinese tea, I asked if we could make use of the three hours to see something of Shih-chia-chuang. I remembered coming to this place some fifty years ago when it was a small country town. Now it has become the capital city of Hopeh Province with a big population working and living in the area and many factories, including seven large cotton mills. The soil and climate of Hopeh Province are good for cotton growing. Each mill employs forty or fifty thousand workers. Shih-chia-chuang has many straight and wide thoroughfares with trees lining both sides and also trees down the center. Many people were working and cycling and there was a strong sense of movement and prosperity in the air. I felt happy to have come to see this capital with its very new face.

Wang Pao-fu, who came in the car with us, suggested we go to see the tomb of the late Dr. Norman Bethune in the Central Park. Dr. Bethune was a Canadian who came to join the Chinese Red Army and traveled with them for several thousand miles in order to give medical help to the soldiers. He died a martyr at his post in 1939. Chairman Mao wrote a famous essay, "In Memory of Norman Bethune," in which he praised the Canadian doctor's international spirit, utter devotion to others, selflessness, responsibility, warmheartedness, constancy, purity, and moral integrity. He is buried in the center of the Shih-chia-chuang public park and many flowers are constantly laid there by the local people. I stood a minute in silence, admiring his sacrifice for the Chinese.

We then returned to the station to catch our train for Chengchow. On the move once more, I stood near the train window to look at the country scenes of the north China plain. It was the middle of May and, although spring came to the north a little later than in central China and the south, most of the fields and trees were covered in young green. All the years I spent in Europe and America, I was confined to the towns and cities and seldom had much chance to see such open green spaces, with many people busy in them. Gazing at them gave me much satisfaction on this trip of return to my homeland. In the south of Hopeh, Yang Shu-tien told me, much irrigation work had been done since 1966 in order to control the flooding of the Huai River which runs through a large area of central China. I then hoped to find time to have a look at the Huai.

Fan Fu-yun, from the Chengchow branch of the China Travel Service, was there to take us to the hotel and after dinner a plan was drawn up for our going to see the Yellow River the next morning. The car was ready early to take the five of us to Hua-yuan-kou, the famous spot which in 1938 the leader

A Chinese countryside scene in spring.

of the Nationalist army ordered to be bombed so as to cut off the advance of
the main Japanese invading force and allow the Nationalist army to escape.
Though this desperate act achieved its purpose of making the Japanese change
their route, the rushing waters from the Yellow River thus released from the
bombed spot poured over forty counties and drowned, it is estimated, some
sixty or seventy thousand people, with many thousands more rendered homeless. The leaders of the Nationalist army showed no remorse for their evil action. The bombed part of the dyke was carefully pointed out to me by my
companions, who later took me to see the actual marks where the new stone
dyke had been built to enclose the gap at Hua-yuan-kou. The new dyke with
its stones cut by hand extended twenty miles or so. No one would believe it
could have been accomplished without the help of any machinery.

Men and women moving stones and rocks to be used for building a dam.

I had never seen "China's Sorrow" (as the Yellow River was called in
the West) before. Like many other Chinese, I had read in my younger days
how the earliest Chinese civilization arose near the valley of the Yellow
River. So many early writings, particularly poetry, have spoken of this Yellow River; it stirred deep feelings to see it now. This part of the Yellow River
at Hua-yuan-kou is very wide; the opposite bank was seen as a mere thin line.
The wide expanse of the water surface, with much sandy marsh and silt,
stretched as far as the eye could see with no boat or any living thing visible.
A great silence hung over everything. My mind went back to our ancient history and I tried to visualize how the people lived nearby in those days. The
Yellow River is now well-controlled and has not flooded for the past twenty
years or so. Instead its waters have been diverted to irrigate practically the
whole Chiliying area, a little way north of Chengchow. It is now a beneficial
river, no more "China's Sorrow."

I remembered a curious touching story that I heard in Canberra, Australia, about the youngest daughter of my good friend Wang Hsin-wu, the librarian in charge of the Chinese Section in the National Library of Australia. When her mother and elder sister made a trip to China, she asked them only to bring back for her some water from the Yellow River, no other present. This young girl, called Chu-sun, was not born on Chinese soil, but her reading of Chinese history had made a deep impression on her mind about the Yellow River. I had a good dinner in her house and she showed me the tiny bottle of water from the Yellow River. How moving was this love for the country to which she and her parents belonged. I could not forget it, so I walked down to the edge to touch the water of the Yellow River myself.

Afterward I was taken to see the Honan Provincial Museum where Han Shao-shih showed me round the many glass cases of newly excavated objects, for Honan Province, like Shensi, had been the ancient seat of government for many centuries and its earth is rich in hidden treasures. In recent years, over ten thousand art objects have come to light, so many that the museum had no room to show them all. I was particularly struck by two enormous square tings (a bronze vessel on four legs). They were cast in the Shang dynasty. One is slightly larger than the other (the larger is 100 centimeters high, mouth length 60.8 centimeters, mouth width 62.5 centimeters, depth 46 centimeters, and weight 164.8 pounds—lighter than the San-mu-wu ting). Both were unearthed at Chang-chai, South Street, Chengchow, in 1974. I wondered for what purpose the Shang rulers had ordered such a big and heavy vessel to be cast, whether it would be heaped with beef or mutton on a sacrificial day. Where it was to be placed and many other points need to be studied carefully.

In the same museum there was a section on the history of the Yellow River. Chao Hsueh-ying showed me around this and provided a lucid and careful explanation which made many points clear to me. I used to think the frequent floods were caused by the melting of snows on the Himalaya mountains. But it is not so; there is a big rain belt in the upper valley where torrential rainfall regularly caused the river to overflow its banks for miles. The Yellow River originates in the northern foothills of the Bayan Kara Mountains in Tsinghai Province and flows forty-eight hundred kilometers through Tsinghai, Szechüan, Kansu, Ningsia, Inner Mongolia, Shensi, Shansi, Honan, and Shantung to empty into the Po Hai, the Yellow Sea.

After seeing the museum, I was taken to a new excavation at Ta-ho-ts'un, not far away from the city. I was told the site had been discovered when one of the local peasants was ploughing a field and struck something like a pottery jar. He immediately reported it to the leader of his commune. Soon some archaeologists arrived to make a systematic excavation. It turned out to be the site of an ancient community dating back some fifty-five hundred years. It was quite a large site, of the Neolithic period, and only a part has been uncovered so far. This part has been roofed over with a modern structure like the Pan P'o site in Shensi. (Ta-ho-ts'un is said to be five hundred years later

Ploughing a rice field with a water buffalo.

than Pan P'o.) The rooms of a house are clearly distinguishable and many pottery urns and pots have been recovered, some of them with painted designs similar to though not quite the same as those from Pan P'o. Not far from the site of the house, two square pits had been dug and several workers were searching for fresh discoveries. A few human skulls had been uncovered but some of the remaining skeletons were still covered with earth. A difference between the sites is that at Pan P'o men and women were not buried together, whereas the graves were found together at Ta-ho-ts'un. Within the five hundred years, what may have been a matriarchal society seems to have changed to a patriarchal one.

In the afternoon I went to have a look at the Chengchow ceramic factory, for the Tz'u-chou ware of the Sung dynasty in Honan Province was most famous. Though the designs of present-day Chengchow ware do not bear any similarity to the ancient pieces, the clay, found locally, and the technique seem to be much the same. I was interested to meet Pai Wen-min, the technical superintendent of the factory, who told me that he spent a number of years in Ching-te-chen of my native province Kiangsi, which had been the ceramic center of China for many centuries.

Along the street a new textile printing and dyeing factory caught my attention and we went in for a look. The work processes did not differ much from the same type of factory in Europe and America, though it was much smaller in scale and the decorative designs printed on the cloth were typically Chinese, both traditional and new in motif. We also went up the Twin-Top Pagoda, a memorial to many laborers who were massacred by the war lord Wu P'ai-fu during the great labor strike of February 1, 1923. From the very top we had a bird's eye view of the whole city of Chengchow, with its many side streets and factory chimneys indicating it was a modern industrial city.

VII

Moving Southward

FROM CHENGCHOW, Yang Shu-tien accompanied me on my southward journey. We reached Nanking by train in the morning. Spring was in full bloom and there were green leaves and red buds on the peach trees. When feeling homesick in London in 1934, I wrote, 春來無夢不江南, "Chun lai wu meng pu chiang nan," which means "When spring comes, every dream takes me back to the south of the River [Yangtze]." I had read this line over and over again during the past forty-odd years and now I was in fact south of the Yangtze.

Nanking was also an ancient capital of China with many historical sites. I had studied in the National Southeastern University in Nanking for four years; many beautiful spots brought memories of my student days, though great changes and restorations had taken place. I went to see the newly created Tai-ping-tien-kuo Memorial Hall, at Yu-hua-tai, the Terrace of Flowering Rain. Yu-hua-tai used to be a wide-open space with masses of small pebbles; it must have been a seashore millions of years ago. Many curio collectors used to search for unusual pebbles there. I did too on many occasions in my student days. The leader of the Tai-ping Rebellion, Hung Hsiu-chuan, had incited a mass of hard-pressed peasants from the southwest to rise up against the Manchus in 1851. The original movement was a good one, with the purpose of land reform and land redistribution, but Hung's ideas were distorted by combination with a not clearly understood kind of Protestant Christianity. And he and his followers were not in accord in working out a logical system of government. The general mass of the peasants remained illiterate and blind worship brought an inevitable failure.

My happiest moments in Nanking were meeting a few of my old classmates like Tseng Shih-yu, who majored in chemistry; Hsu Man-ying and Mao Li-kung, mathematics students; and Fan Tseng-chung who majored in English literature, later earned a Ph.D. in England, and is now the head of Nanking University. The present Nanking University is a combination of the former three universities—Nanking University for Men, Nanking Women's University, and the National Southeastern University, a coeducational school. We were all over seventy now and we had some good laughs when we talked about our japes in the classrooms and dormitories in our younger days. Dr. Fan had the kindness to spare some of his precious time to show me round a few of the new buildings and chat with me about the new higher education system. He asked a colleague to explain to me that there was no examination for entrance to colleges and universities. Every youngster after graduation from the middle school could express a wish to do advanced studies in colleges and universities, but he or she must first have at least two years of experience either in a commune or factory. Their work would then be estimated by their fellow workers before they could be recommended to the

A young girl working in a rice field.

local authority for advanced studies. Those who were approved would be asked to go for interviews with administrative personnel and professors of the specialized subjects they wanted to study. I expressed my agreement with the abolition of entrance examinations, but I wondered if some good students might not have missed the chance for recommendation and approval. Dr. Fan agreed that there could be such a possibility but, since all the proceedings were carried out with the utmost care, it would only happen rarely. The only trouble they had now was that some professors who had little commune or factory experience found difficulty in answering practical questions. Therefore several noted universities in China had also set up small factories within their campuses.

In my student years I had spent many hours walking round and about a particular ancient tree, said to have been planted in the fourth century A.D. I wanted to see if it was still flourishing. Yang Shu-tien, Chu Chuan-chih, from the local China Travel Service, and I eventually found the *liu-chao-sung,* or "pine of the six-dynasties period," still alive and looking much as it had in my university days. Yang and Chu took some photographs of us with the old tree and I made a quick sketch and composed a simple verse:

朝　依　色　處　舊　往　存　卅
松　然　相　處　踪　昔　忠　年
　　古　　都　成　成　　不
　　老　　呈　賢　賢　　見
　　六　　新　認　認　　范

A reunion with Dr. Fan after thirty years!
The old Cheng-hsien Street has many of our footprints.
Everywhere shows a new look,
But the ancient, rugged *liu-chao-sung* is still the same.*

The six-dynasties pine at Nanking University.

*I had seen Dr. Fan in London after World War II ended in 1945. Our students' dormitory was on Cheng-hsien Street.

Next morning I went to see the Nanking Museum which had been established in 1951 under the direction of the late Tseng Chao-yueh whom I had known very well, for we stayed in London at the same time. She was well-versed in Chinese history and literature but came to study archaeology under the late Professor Percevall Yetts at the Courtauld Institute. She went back to China during the Japanese invasion; I heard from her at long intervals while the war was on. I later heard that she was making good use of what she had studied in England and was doing excellent work in directing excavations and arranging museums after the liberation. I longed to see the museum she had established and wanted to meet her again; unfortunately she had passed away from hard work two years before my arrival. A young woman, Tsu Chang-yu, who showed us round, said that nothing special had been set up in her memory in the museum, although they all missed her personally. However, I felt happy to have come to see most of the exhibits she had handled herself. Forty-two years ago there had been no museum for students like us. Now this museum not only was of good size but was full of interesting old relics for study. Like many others, the museum had so many objects it could not display them all at once. This is one of the astonishing achievements of the new government within only twenty-five years.

One of my nieces, Tsai Ching-yung, a retired army nurse, was living in Nanking with her husband, Tung Yu-hsi, a retired Red Army man who was wounded during the civil war. They have an only son, Hsiao-chun, twenty years old, who studied ivory and jade carving after graduation from the middle school. As he is the only son of the family, he was allowed to work in Nanking and lives at home. My two daughters, Hsiao-yen and Chien-lan, with their husbands were all in Nanking now, so as to be with me as much as possible. The eight of us, including Yang Shu-tien, went on an excursion to see the tomb of the first emperor of the Ming dynasty, Chu Hung-wu, the Ling-ku Monastery, and also Dr. Sun Yat-sen's Tomb, three famous sights on the same road.

Dr. Sun's tomb was built after I had graduated from the university and left Nanking. So this was my first visit. I admired the setting of the tomb with its grand view into the far distance. The blue-glazed roof tiles made an admirable color scheme with the white marble balustrades beside the several hundred stone steps, the green trees, and the rosy-red peach blossoms just in bloom. This is a most successful and beautiful piece of modern Chinese architecture (finished in 1934). In this century a number of good Chinese scholars have specialized in architecture and the late Lu Nien-chin was one of them. Lu sent in his design to the competition for the construction of a tomb for Dr. Sun Yat-sen while he was still studying in America. After his design had been accepted, he came to Nanking to supervise its construction. Unfortunately he died of cancer without being able to see his monumental work completed. That was more than forty years ago. Since the setting up of the new govern-

Dr. Sun Yat-sen's mausoleum in Nanking.

ment in Peking in 1949, a few important buildings have been constructed in Peking, such as the Great Hall of the People and the Workers' Stadium, the round structure of which, with a stream of water surrounding it, is quite pleasing and satisfying to the eye.

A modern stadium for workers in Peking.

Early next morning, Hsiao-chun came to see me off. As there was time to spare before I set out for my next destination, we went to see the famous Nanking Bridge over the Yangtze. We were well received by the young woman in charge, Chu Hsiu-mei and two of her staff. For years since my university days there had been talk of building this bridge. The river is wide and fast-flowing at this point; in the old days when I used to cross the river on a steamer, it took about an hour. Some Western engineers and advisers thought its construction would be impossible. They said that any attempt would be doomed to failure. Despite all this, Chairman Mao's words gave such impetus to Chinese engineers and workers that with collective spirit eventually they got this bridge finished. A well-known Chinese saying, "Nothing is difficult under heaven if you make up your mind to do it" proved true for the Nanking Bridge.

In the afternoon, Chu Chuan-chih made arrangement for us to see Yang-chou. I was delighted at the suggestion for I had never been there before, though I knew Soochow and Hangchow quite well. This visit would fulfill a long-cherished hope. We went by car and reached our destination before dusk. Yin Chih-lan, in charge of Yang-chou, took us to a hotel quite close to the famous Su-hsi-hu, or Slender West Lake. Perhaps it was so-called to distinguish it from the rounder, famous West Lake of Hangchow. It was still light and we walked slowly along the bank of the slender lake. A faint new moon was rising; it reflected in the lake quite clearly. Yin Chih-lan explained

Old-style pushcarts in Yang-chou, Kiangsu.

to us when we walked near the Five-Arbor Bridge that at midnight a full moon could be seen from beneath the fifteen arches as if there were fifteen moons. How could it be so? I could not imagine it. In the distance I noticed a white stupa, similar to the one in the Peking Palace, reflected in the water.

A white stupa in Peking Palace.

This had been specially built to please the Emperor Chien-lung when he came to the south for a visit. The local people had to spend so much in preparation for entertaining the emperor in those days that they were driven almost to bankruptcy. But as it turned out on that occasion, the emperor did not even come to Yang-chou and all that money and labor were spent for no purpose. That kind of waste occurred many a time in the long history of China.

I asked about the work of the well-known 揚州八怪, *Yang-chou Pa kuai*, or the "eight eccentrics of Yang-chou"—eight important painters of the eighteenth century. Their work had been collected feverishly by friends in their lifetime, and sold too. There was no museum or gallery to house them in Yang-chou; some of their paintings are in the Nanking and Peking museums.

Then we came to a pavilion built near the lake that had a number of miniature trees and flowering shrubs arranged in beautiful pottery pots which attracted me particularly. They were similar to what the Japanese call bonzai, yet not quite the same. One of the pots contained a flowering shrub called *liu-yueh-hseuh,* or "June snow," and another had a miniature tree called *pa-yang-shu,* or "dreading-to-be-touched tree," for its leaves all closed as soon as it was touched. On leaving the pavilion, I composed a short verse:

勤　來　自　江　添　風　幾　五　瘦
勞　看　力　州　一　騷　經　亭　西
・　農　今　老　怪　！　八　橋　湖
　　工　朝　，　，　　　怪　，　，
　　畢　；　　　　　　　弄

The slender West Lake,
The Five-Arbor Bridge,
How many times did the eight eccentrics play their antics here?
Now comes one more eccentric,
A man of Chiang-chow,
Working with self-reliance in the present century,
Coming to see the peasants and laborers industriously at work.

The next spot we came to was called Ping-shan-tan, or Level-with-the-Mountain Hall, so named by Ou-yang Hsiu, a great scholar of the Sung dynasty who had been a governor of the city and happened to be a Kiangsi man like me. From the middle of the hall one's eye seemed to be at the same

level as the distant mountain ranges; hence the name. Afterward we came to
the Chien-chen-tang, or Hall of Monk Chien-chen, with a lacquered portrait
of the monk such as I had seen in Nara, Japan. I told the story of Chien-chen
in my book *The Silent Traveller in Japan*:

> Chien-chen was born in 688 and was ordained a monk at fourteen at the
> Ta-yun Monastery in Yangchow of Kiangsu province. He later went north
> to make further study of Buddhism in Lo-yang as well as in Ch'ang-an
> under many famous priests. Apart from his knowledge of Buddhism, he ex-
> celled in the study of Chinese architecture and also in medicine. Within ten
> years he became widely known as the leader of the Chinese Buddhist re-
> ligion. In 733 the emperor Shomu Tenna of Japan sent the priests Eiei of
> Kofukuji and Fucu of Ran-an-jito to invite Chien-chen to come to Japan.
> At that time the sea voyage was dreaded by many. Chien-chen had no
> response from his disciples so he decided to lead the expedition himself.
> He made preparation with the help of the two Japanese monks and gathered
> more than a hundred and eighty persons including artists, jade carvers,
> wood and stone engravers and embroiderers and bought a large ship for the
> trip. Unfortunately they encountered a strong wind and the ship ran
> aground on a small island. They suffered hardship: the winter of 743 was
> an especially bitter one. . . .

Chien-chen met a smiliar fate on the next four attempts, but he was undaunted in spirit. He eventually arrived at Nara and the Japanese, from the
emperor down to the humblest subject, gave him a great welcome and treated
him as the most honored foreign guest, with the deepest reverence. I was
happy to have come to the hall where Chien-chen used to stay some twelve
hundred years ago. I could see from what the new China has achieved that
the Chinese still possess an undaunted spirit.

I had another reason for coming to see Yang-chou besides exploring its
beauties. Yang-chou had in the past often suffered from the flooding of the
nearby Huai River. When Chairman Mao issued the great call in 1951 that the
Huai River must be harnessed, all the people living within reach of the river
responded collectively, for they realized that to rid themselves of their former
suffering was in their own hands. The work was eventually accomplished by
several tens of thousands of people working together on a river-control project. Two large locks, Wan-fu-cha and Tai-ping-cha, were shown to me.
Through a glass structure inside the tower of the last lock I could see many
fish swimming to and fro the entire length of the lock without any hindrance.
With the water control in hand, the irrigation of the rice fields in the area
benefited greatly too. Thus the yearly rice production increased enormously. I
also saw a big reservoir in the process of being built with hundreds of people,
men and women, working side by side. As in other places, they built and
worked with their own bare hands.

Though the time for my stay in China was limited, before moving south, I felt I must see Shanghai while I was in the vicinity. So we went back to Nanking by car and on to Shanghai by train. I had particular reasons for wanting to see Shanghai, where I had spent a year and half, from 1926 to 1928, with many unhappy experiences. Shanghai was then known to the world as the greatest industrial and commercial center in the Far East. To other countries Shanghai was then the most important city in China, but no one ever thought of mentioning that this great industrial and commercial center was not run by the Chinese themselves but by the Westerners. On the east bank of the Huang-P'u River were many cotton mills, chiefly owned by the Japanese and English, as well as many other light industries; very few of these were owned by the Chinese.

Most of the foreign-owned factories could not recruit workers themselves but relied on local Chinese who had picked up some pidgin English and had become *kung-tou,* or "foremen." As the foreign employers seldom tried to learn Chinese, they relied on these *kung-tou,* who could do as they pleased with those who applied for jobs. They demanded heavy bribes before they would engage applicants; they even tried to squeeze some of the workers' miserable wages. They worked out various scales of wages with their bosses but never paid the workers accordingly. They created serious injustices behind the backs of their foreign bosses. During my time in Shanghai, factory strikes occurred one after another, but the foreign owners never took the trouble to find out the source of the unrest.

In those days in Shanghai, anyone who could speak a few words of English could consider himself superior, for he might be able to make a deal with foreigners or be employed by foreign concerns. Nearly every big business concern or department store had its building inside the international settlement.

Modern Huang-P'u River scene in Shanghai.

Outside the settlement was the Chinese city where only small concerns and department stores were set up. Like the factory owners, the heads of these big business concerns and department stores knew very little Chinese; they employed some English-speaking Chinese as go-betweens. These go-betweens formed a new class in China known as compradors—a new word in the English dictionary. The compradors squeezed commissions from both sides—from their foreign employers and from the Chinese merchants who wanted to make deals with the foreigners. Gradually this comprador class became richer, bigger, and more powerful. Their support was eventually sought by the war lords as well as the high officials in the central government in Nanking, for both needed to borrow money for their projects and plans. Many compradors slowly found their ways into government, and this produced an evil influence on the whole Chinese economy.

Under the unequal treaties, foreign boats, even gunboats, could sail into the interior of China. So I often saw the Huang P'u River at Shanghai full of foreign boats of different sizes with the flags of many countries at their mastheads. Their crews would pour onto the shore in search of pleasure. Some might buy souvenirs but most went to the street girls. Prostitution flourished in Shanghai more than in any other city in China then. There was a special type of prostitute there, waiting for the foreign sailors along the Pa-hsien-chiao, or the Eight-Immortals Bridge, and in its neighborhood. These women did not wear Chinese gowns but went about almost half-naked. In those days the plague of venereal disease was widespread. The Shanghai newspapers were full of advertisements for the cure of such diseases, as if Shanghai doctors were experts in that particular branch of medicine.

After my arrival this time, I asked to be taken to that former evil district and was happy to see all was changed; not one prostitute or any beggars in sight. Where have all those people gone to? Many died, no doubt, but I was told that many of the girls had married, borne children, and were working in the factories. And some of the beggars, the surviving ones, were working in the factories too. How could I fail to marvel at the remarkable achievement of reforming those people within so short a time—only twenty-five years.

There were no foreign boats on the Huang P'u River any more and Shanghai is now China's leading industrial city with all the factories run by the government. I also went to the Shanghai Exhibition Hall which displayed all China-made products, some for heavy industry and some for light. A good many China-made cars and tractors were on display and I was told that the Hai-ou, or "seagull," cameras produced in Shanghai were in great demand both for export and for home consumption.

I have many friends and old classmates still living in Shanghai but I only had time to see two of them. One was my former chemistry-laboratory assistant, Dr. Chang Chiang-shu, now head of the Shanghai Chemical Engineering College, who received me with a broad smile; he well remembered, years ago, correcting my chemistry-laboratory reports. We talked about China's new higher education system in some detail. He particularly pointed out that in our university days when many of us wanted to do advanced studies in science, there was no proper laboratory equipment for it. So most promising students went abroad to continue their studies. When they finished, they could not find suitable employment in China, so they remained working abroad. Nowadays students no longer need to go abroad for study and many factories employ science students as soon as they have completed their university work.

In fact, a good many Chinese universities have a factory on the campus and factories have university courses too. For instance, the Shanghai Machine Tool Factory conducts courses in trigonometry, mechanical design, hydraulics, and a few other practical subjects for forty or fifty workers who attend the courses for three years and draw their working salary at the same time. In

A peasant reading in the field.

this way higher education has become a useful social and economic means to combine study and production. In addition, some universities, including the Fu-tan University at Shanghai, have established many university correspondence courses for factory workers and peasants on communes. Even if they are not able to attend a university, they can study on their own and acquire the theoretical knowledge needed for their particular work. This keeps the university, the factory or commune, and society together as three in one.

Dr. Chang told me that his college had just set up a new department for petroleum research to solve China's problem of much-needed energy. China had discovered and developed many new oil fields such as those at Ta-ching and Ta-chen. So far the oil flow from China's own oil fields is more than enough for her own consumption; the surplus is exported to her neighbors. This was something I had never dreamed of when I was in China forty-two years ago.

Another old friend of mine I wanted to see in Shanghai was Professor Liu Hai-su, a great artist, now eighty years of age. When he was in his twenties, he established a College of Fine Arts in Shanghai. The college was divided into two departments, one for the study of traditional Chinese painting and the other for the study of Western art, including anatomy and sculpture. Life study was something entirely new in Shanghai then and when Professor Liu tried to find a life model, no Chinese, not even a prostitute, would take the job. Eventually a French girl came from the French concession. This roused a great storm of protest from the old school of Confucianists, with their strict, narrow morality. They said that it would lead to all kinds of evils in society. They influenced the war lord Sun Chuan-fang to issue a warrant for Professor Liu's arrest. But he managed to get away in time to Japan. Kou Mo-jo once wrote the following poem on one of his paintings:

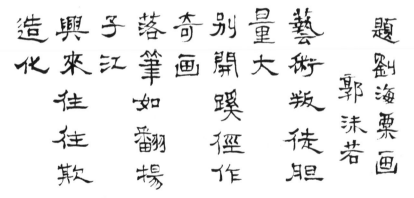

The art-rebel, whose bravery is great,
Creates his work in nontraditional manner with special taste.
When he sets down his brush, he seems to turn the Yangtze River upside down.
When inspired, he often cheats the ontology of nature.

I met Professor Liu in London in 1934 when he brought an exhibition of contemporary Chinese paintings to show in several European cities. Though we continued our correspondence after he returned to Shanghai in 1935, we lost touch with one another when Japan invaded China. It was a great joy to see him again after nearly half a century. He looked the same energetic person at eighty. He has been painting for the past years despite all kinds of difficult conditions. He took out many of his works which I had not seen before. Each had immense vitality in the brush strokes. His unswerving energy and industriousness had kept his vigor alive. Painting, like any other form of art, has to be practiced continuously for the sake of improving expression, yet more than other forms of art it needs a creative impulse as well. Afterward I invited him and Mrs. Liu, also a painter, to my hotel for dinner. We ordered a special, seasonal dish of *shih-yu,* a fish similar to the American shad, which appears in the lower part of the Yangtze River near Shanghai in May and June. It was cooked in the Shanghai style—tasty and juicy; I had not eaten it since I left China. This made our meeting even more enjoyable that evening.

VIII

Home at Last

NOW IT WAS time for me to fulfill my great longing to see my home cities. My birthplace was Kiukiang but my elder daughter, her children, and her invalid mother were living in Nan-ch'ang, capital of Kiangsi Province. In my university days I used to enjoy traveling from Kiukiang by a big river steamboat to Nanking, which then continued to its terminal at Shanghai. So I asked Yang Shu-tien to book a berth on the river boat for me so that I could see once again all the familiar scenery along the Yangtze River, upstream from Shanghai to Kiukiang. As China is an absolutely independent country now, the old river-steamer companies, two English and the other Japanese, had long disappeared. The only one now operating, a Chinese company, was fully booked with no suitable berth for me, Yang Shu-tien told me. He suggested that I should first take the train from Shanghai to Nan-ch'ang and then from Nan-ch'ang to Kiukiang. Formerly there had been no direct rail link between Shanghai and Nan-ch'ang. I was told that many more railroads had been built in the past twenty years or so and many places were now accessible by train. This was a great improvement for China, an enormous country, long in need of good communications to connect cities and provinces and reduce the former isolation which encouraged the activities of war lords and also increased the diversity of local dialects.

I told Yang Shu-tien that it would suit me very well to go first to Nan-ch'ang and see my family sooner. Being the capital of Kiangsi Province where the provincial governor's office was and where all his subordinates lived, Nan-ch'ang was where I used to come to for consultation during my term of office in Kiukiang. But I never liked to stay there, for the head of the provincial government at that time was not interested in talking about the local matters. What he and his subordinates were doing mostly was enjoying social calls and entertainments. I often wondered what he considered his duties to be. The central government then had no real control over the different provinces. If the provincial governor paid no attention to what the county governor had suggested for the local people nothing ever got done.

I remember a comic event when the head of the Kiangsi provincial government, General Hsiung Shih-hui, tried to spread Chiang Kai-shek's policy of the so-called New Life Movement. This included ordering people to dress neatly, never considering that many peasants had hardly anything to wear at all. The governor's official residence, or *yamen* in Chinese, was always guarded by two soldiers posted on each side of the gate. One day a visitor came to see him, wearing a Western-type overcoat with wide lapels. The guards were countryfolk who had never seen a Western overcoat; they insisted that the visitor button up his collar before he was admitted. This caused quite a row. The provincial governor soon became the butt of the Shanghai journalists as one who thought that buttoning up coat lapels neatly meant new life for China.

On my arrival at Nan-ch'ang station, my elder daughter, her husband, and their five children, together with a number of other relations, were there to meet me. My eyes grew wet, for the acute pain of the bitter-and-sweet sensation I had experienced when I first met my two daughters in Peking had risen again in me. My legs felt weak but, being a strong-willed person, I tried to control my emotions and smile at the many relations whom I had not seen for more than forty years. My elder daughter and her husband have their living quarters in a school hostel. Though it was not too big, they had invited relations from other places to meet me and they all had to stay together. My younger daughter and her husband had also come from Peking to join the family party, as did my niece from Nanking and my sister's daughter from Kiukiang. Their home was full, with the invalid mother, my wife, occupying one room. The local China Travel Service had booked me a room in a local hotel.

As soon as I had deposited my luggage in the hotel room, I asked to be motored to see my invalid wife who had lived with our elder daughter since the latter had married. My wife had contracted an incurable disease after giving birth to our last child. As she was feeble in her limbs and unable to write, we did not have much direct news of one another after I was forced to leave China for England. My two girls were very young then; one five and the other only two. There were so many things I wanted to ask about how they had managed to survive for all the past years.

The local Revolutionary Committee, together with Red Army personnel, found out that my elder brother and I had been Nationalist officials. They investigated whether my brother and I had accumulated any wealth or property. We had none, so they looked after my children's education. Although many of my relations and friends seemed to have died from advanced age or disease, none of them as far as I heard at the time, was killed by the revolutionary forces or during the civil war. It puzzled me that many Western reports in the newspapers claimed that the revolutionary forces had killed millions of people.

A thousand and one things all came into my mind at once and I could not ask a single question at first. It was utterly unimaginable to me how my long-invalided wife could have endured so many years of being bedridden. She had to be carried into meals by the elder granddaughter. All the time I sat there looking at everyone, I had acute pain inside me, yet I could not show it in my face, for this reunion of us all was a miracle such as I had never dreamed of. After dinner I stayed on till the late hours. Fortunately my five grandchildren, the youngest of

whom was only eleven years old, kept me occupied with one story after another
and they could all sing too. So the whole afternoon and evening passed. My head
was full of thoughts and became even more so when I returned to the hotel. I
could not sleep at all the whole night. I thought of my many friends in Europe
and America who always regarded me as a happy-go-lucky man. None of them
imagined what I had been through in my forty-two years outside China.

Next morning I was taken to Nan-ch'ang Hospital to have some dentures as arranged from Peking. My teeth had never been good. During the war years when I
lived in England I was advised by my dentist there to have all my bad teeth taken
out. He made a set of false teeth, but for some unknown reason they cracked after
a few years. I had a new set made in Hong Kong which did not fit too badly.
Later I should have liked to get a better set made in New York, but the cost was
too prohibitive. While I was preparing my trip to China many friends suggested
that I should have a new set made in Peking, for China's medical work has
achieved a great reputation in recent years. So I went to make arrangements with
a dentist in Peking Hospital. I was told it would take at least a month, for in Peking many visitors from abroad came to that hospital for treatment; it was so good
and cheaper than anywhere else in the world. I myself saw the waiting rooms
filled with patients. I asked Yang Shu-tien and also my elder son-in-law if they
could make some arrangement with a dentist in Nan-ch'ang Hospital to have a set
of teeth made there. This was arranged, and I therefore came to the Hospital of
Nan-ch'ang Medical College.

An old dentist at work.

Three doctors responsible for the administration of the college and four dental
specialists met me there. Following a thorough examination of my mouth, some

plastic molds were made of my upper and lower jaws. Afterward we were entertained with tea and some interesting talk. I felt overwhelmed by their kindness
and my mind went back a good many years, remembering the ill-equipped conditions in the old Nan-ch'ang Hospital. The present hospital is a branch of the
Kiangsi Medical College and all the doctors and specialists there teach as well as
attend to patients. Most of the equipment is new since 1949 and its work is
inspected and checked every week by responsible representatives of the provincial government. All the doctors and hospital workers attend conferences from
time to time to discuss matters concerning one another's work and how to improve upon it if necessary. The financial side is seen to by the government, while
the doctors concentrate on their teaching and medical treatments. The doctors
who took part in our conversation expressed their pleasure in their work, for they
were all given a free hand to do their best and were proud of being able to serve
the people. The dentist who took care of my teeth was a woman, Dr. Li Shou-i.
After the first treatment I went to my daughter's home for a meal with my wife
and children.

In the past I remembered the streets of Nan-ch'ang as narrow and always
crowded with a great hubbub of people talking as loudly as if their companions
were deaf. Now the streets are wider, particularly in the newly built housing
areas for workers and factory people. Nan-ch'ang did not have factories in the
past, but now there are many scattered around the suburbs. Like many other
provincial capitals, this city has expanded enormously. It has a big city square
in the center where large crowds could gather for a conference or celebration.
A new provincial museum had been set up too, facing the square.

I was lucky to arrive in Nan-ch'ang when a province-wide exhibition of paintings by school children had just opened. My elder daughter's four girls took me
all through the exhibition, among thousands of other young children, and showed
good taste in their judgment. The eldest, Wei-wei, is nearly twenty and has been
working in an agricultural commune for a few years. She is now studying in a
College for Hygiene and Social Welfare. She is robust and strong, able to carry a
hundred-pound load on her shoulders as if it were a trifle. She really represents
the young people who have grown up with the revolution. Her conversation has
much to do with her training and that of her generation—the growing of food and
producing of machinery to build up the new nation. I seldom tried to cut in while
she was talking but felt amazed at how the youngsters talked so differently and so
much more freely than when I was their age. The second, Ni-ni, and the third,
Ting-ting, both graduated at the same time and had been waiting to be assigned
work in a commune or factory. They told me that according to the government's
policy one of them should get work near the parents' home and the two of them
need never be away at the same time. Eventually the second one was given work
in a city factory, not far from her parents' home, so she could help her mother at
times. She is quite literary in inclination and loves writing and calligraphy; she
urged the others to learn calligraphy from me. The fourth, Ling-ling, is about to

A young girl learning calligraphy.

enter a middle school; she is strong and loves gymnastics and sports. She was once first in throwing a discus among thousands of school children from the whole province. The fifth, Ding-ding, is an eleven-year-old boy with a ready smile; he loves doing mechanical work. These five kept me from having a dull moment.

In fact, they surprised me more than anything else I had seen in China during the previous month. They made me recall my younger days as an orphan, without a mother at five and later no father. I received little attention from my uncle and aunt who took over the running of our big household after my grandmother's death. They never wanted to pay for my school fees and I had no guidance from anyone. But these five youngsters studied all through elementary school, went on to middle school, and then went to work in the commune or factory, all of which were well arranged by the government. They know far more about study and work than I did at their age. They are very lucky. With these five youngsters around me day after day, I naturally felt my age but was happy to see in them the future of China. All of their talk represents the new generation of China, free and outspoken with not a bit of the shyness I had in my younger days. They are going to keep China progressive through the future, I am sure.

From time to time I could not help remembering how I used to walk around with my old grandfather some sixty years ago. My grandfather never bothered about how I felt about things, but just expressed his own comments. I, as a youngster in those days, was always in an obedient mood, expressing no personal feelings at all. As a matter of fact, I never felt that I had anything to say. Nowadays young children have more individuality and can express their opinions freely. With my grandchildren I felt no generation gap and we enjoyed each other's comments. However, they had not entirely discarded the old ways, for they are very much attached to the home and bound by family affection.

Two of my old companions from Kiukiang middle school days came to see me and had lunch at my hotel. I had not seen them for more than half a century. One was P'an Heng, who had been the headmaster of two middle schools and was now retired, and the other, Dr. Kuo Pai-han, a well-known physician specializing in Chinese medicine had now joined the Provincial Hospital in Nan-ch'ang. P'an was one year younger and Dr. Kuo five years younger than I. We three had so much to say about the past but I always led them on to tell me more about their lives after I left China. P'an Heng still attached himself to local education in some way and told me he found that the new generation received a more thorough education than before, for the local government kept a watch on their improvement very keenly and very few students were left idle. Sports and swimming were encouraged, as they were not in my young days. Dr. Kuo Pai-han said that he was asked in Kiukiang to join the Provincial Hospital in Nan-ch'ang and was very well treated and respected by all those above him. He only had to attend the hospital three days a week and he could do his own research at home unless urgently needed. Both had enjoyed the past twenty-five years of peace, without any worry about getting paid or about food and clothes.

My new set of teeth would take some time to make; I was told to go back to the hospital for a fitting after a few days. So I took the opportunity to see some interesting places near Nan-ch'ang. First I made a two-day journey to Ching-te-chen, the great ceramic center of China, famous since the eleventh century and even earlier. *Ching-te* was one of the *nien-hao,* or "reigning titles," of the Sung emperor Chen-tsung. He ordered it to be put on the bases of the officially manufactured porcelain. The town was therefore known as Ching-te-chen. At first its wares supplied the needs of the imperial court. Not until the beginning of the Ming period did it start trading with the rest of the world. The hills which surround Ching-te-chen far and wide are rich in the materials required by the pot-

A river scene near Ching-te-chen, Kiangsi.

ters: china clay and china stone of various qualities, fire clay for the saggers (cases to protect the porcelain in the kilns), and numerous other materials. Because of the plentiful supply of materials, the town has never stopped manufacturing porcelain.

Ching-te-chen was not yet open to visitors; the railway extension leading to it was not yet finished, and the only way to go was by car. Tao Lo-li, representative of the Nan-ch'ang's China Travel Service, obligingly provided one and he also accompanied Yang Shu-tien and me. Spring was at its height and the rice fields on both sides of the road were full of peasants, men and women, working diligently, planting out the young rice plants now grown to two or three inches. Some were weeding, too, and others were ploughing with their water buffaloes. This country scene, which I had missed for the past forty-two years, pleased my eyes and mind endlessly. The road we drove on was a newly constructed one; at places made simply of soil and gravel. As we approached our destination at dusk, it started to rain hard and the road quickly became muddy. An electric generator somewhere near the Kan River provided power for the street lamps, which were not in existence fifty years ago when I first visited Ching-te-chen.

A Chinese boat sailing on the River Kan, Kiangsi.

As a boy I had often heard about the Ching-te-chen products from my elders and my father on several occasions designed paintings for the big porcelain plates. Kiukiang has long been the exporting center for Ching-te-chen ware and almost every traveler who passed through Kiukiang would buy some of it. When I managed to make a trip to Ching-te-chen from Kiukiang some fifty years ago transport was very primitive. Partly I rode on horseback and partly went on foot, taking five or six days to get there. On that early visit I saw many small kilns owned and run privately and did not find much going on there then. I was also young and had little knowledge of the subject. This time I saw Ching-te-chen in a new light, for it is now a big city, no longer the small town of the old days. All the small kilns had amalgamated into two big factories with materials provided by the state. The state owned all the products and arranged for their sale as well.

Fang Ching-sheng, of the local China Travel Service, and Jao Yu-shan met us at the hotel. After dinner, we were taken to see the first and main ceramic factory, where hundreds of men and women were at work. I sketched quickly and took photographs in the dim light as well, though I had no flash bulbs. In some areas work such as glazing and trimming the edges of the products was done

A ceramist at work in Ching-te-chen, Kiangsi.

mostly by women, while the molding, engraving, and decorating were done by men, though the division of labor was not an absolute one. As for figurines, most of the traditional subjects were discontinued, but personalities and stories of peasants' and workers' struggles were faithfully portrayed with good taste and in vivid action. Some of these new types of ceramic figurines greatly attracted customers and were in demand. I talked to several potters and found that they had had some years of training in an art college; formerly they were only apprenticed and so were unable to break away from tradition. Some of these new potters were young and expressed their wishes to discover or evolve some new techniques.

Most of the traditional types of vases, dishes, pots, bowls, and jars were continued because their shapes and formations were modeled on those of the ancient Shang and Chou bronzes, which could hardly be improved. To my way of thinking, the history of applied art has developed through changes in material but seldom in form. Though the early bronze forms of Shang and Chou were gradually evolved from the Neolithic potteries, it is interesting to see how these shapes and forms came back in clay. Again the traditional Chinese lion-dogs, the covered

A young ceramic worker at Ching-te-chen, Kiangsi.

ginger jars, as well as the *mei-p'ing,* or long-necked flower vases, were being produced in large quantities; apparently they were much in demand. But I examined some of them and found some *mei-p'ings* had new decorations, not painted by hand or engraved, but something in the glaze formed a pattern when taken out of the kilns and cooled quickly. Even modern works by the late painter, Chi Pai-shih, were incorporated into new designs. It all showed that the modern potters at Ching-te-chen were trying to create new things.

Later I was taken to the Research Institute of Pottery and Porcelain—a new establishment—and met Fang Tsung and Chang Ko-tun, with whom I discussed some points about different types of early ceramics and modern ones, too. I asked if the type of porcelain known in the Western world as eggshell—in Chinese, 薄胎瓷, *Po-tai tzu*—was still being made. The answer was affirmative. Then came the explanation that Chinese eggshell procelain began to appear in the Ming dynasty. It was derived and developed from the Ying-ch'ing ware of the northern Sung period which was thin and translucent with a soft and fine finish. The eggshells made in China were often only 0.5 of a millimeter thick, some even less. The design can be clearly seen through the porcelain when light passes through it. Before the eggshell becomes a finished product, it goes through several dozen processes, including mixing the ingredients, shaping the body, glazing, painting, and firing. Because of the very complicated process and the flimsiness of the substance it is easy to break and crack. A single flaw, such

A ceramic painter at Ching-te-chen, Kiangsi.

as unevenness of cutting, impurity of the material, unsuccessful glazing, or a wrong stroke in the painting, and the product is discarded. Afterward I was shown many modern eggshell pieces such as bowls, plates, wine vessels, brush-writing equipment, fish bowls, and vases in different sizes in the Trading Department of the factory. They were all attractive and inviting to my eyes and mind. I eventually bought a set of five pieces of brush-writing equipment for a collector friend of mine in Hong Kong, Professor H. L. Lo, though I was worried about how to get them there in good condition on my way back.

After having seen Ching-te-chen I returned to Nan-ch'ang to have a fitting for my new set of teeth at Nan-ch'ang Hospital. The rest of the day was spent in my daughter's home with my wife and all the relations. My feeling was not as painful as on the first evening and I again became more interested in the behavior and talk of my five grandchildren. Each of them could sing and play one kind of musical instrument or another and I loved to listen to their singing, for the songs had the old tunes, but new content. Many of the songs they sang were sung to me in other places; they were very popular among the new generation of China. These new songs with old tunes had a great function in educating the young and old of China to understand the government's policies and purpose, a very effective weapon.

Before my second fitting for the teeth I had the opportunity to see my birthplace, the city of Kiukiang, where I had been the local governor. The old railroad from Nan-ch'ang to Kiukiang was still running as before but with many renovations. The compartments were kept cleaner and service was good. Kuo Chi-fu and Feng Yen-ling, both from the local administration office, were at the station to meet me. We were then driven to where I was staying. Not far from Kiukiang station I asked the driver to stop for a minute so that I could take a look at Lung-kai-ho, where the Kan-t'ang Lake joins the Yangtze River. It was here that the poet, P'o Chu-i of the T'ang dynasty wrote the famous song about seeing his friend off at a place nearby called P'en-pu-kan. This famous poem has been translated into English by many; the following version by Innes Herdan is a good one:

> By the Hsun-yang river one night I was bidding a friend farewell.
> In the maple leaves and reed heads autumn soughed harshly.
> I, the host, dismounted; my guest was already aboard:
> We poured the wine and wished to drink, but music was missing.
> And the drinking brought no cheer—in gloom we prepared to part;
> Saw only the vague river reaches drenched in moonlight.
> Suddenly from across the water we heard a guitar's sound.
> I forgot to return home and my guest stayed his leaving. . . .
> We hailed her and urged her a thousand times before she would rise and
>   come.
> Still half-concealing her face behind the guitar she carried.
> She moved the pegs and tried the strings with two or three notes.
> Even before the tune came there was passion in the sound. . . .
> Do not go! Sit down and play another tune;
> I will write a poem for you, a "Song of the Guitar."
> Moved by these words of mine she stood awhile.
> Then sat and tore at the strings, drawing a rush of sound.
> Sadder, more sorrowful than the tunes she had played before;
> The whole company hearing it tried to hide their tears.
> And who of us all, do you suppose, wept the most?
> This prefect of Chiang-chow—my blue coat was wet!

This is a long well-composed poem, the story of a singsong girl, who in her young days was admired and much sought after by rich people. Later she married a merchant who always left home on business, making her life sad and miserable. It has been published, read, and memorized by countless Chinese, and Japanese scholars since the eighth century. Most were fascinated by the literary qualities and beauty in reading it, but few questioned why this prefect should feel so sad at holding a post far away from the court. More than a thousand years separated me from P'o-chu-i; I should have lost my small position as the head civil servant of the same place if I had gone to the riverside and enjoyed a girl's playing at that time. Apart from getting a bad name, I should probably have been demoted for neglecting my job. The ancient Chinese officials seemed to be rarely concerned about their tasks in the lands they administered; they preferred to associate themselves with the emperor whether he ruled well or not. The long history of China contains many such examples.

The hotel arranged for my stay formerly housed the administrative offices of a missionary college run by American Christians—where my sister's husband had studied for a year before they were married. About a hundred years ago, after China had signed the unequal treaties with the Western powers, Western missionaries came to China to build schools in treaty ports like Kiukiang. They always chose the best sites, and this former missionary college was built in Western style with large grounds.

After the meal, Kuo Chi-fu and Feng Yen-ling drove Yang Shu-tien and me around the city. Every inch reminded me of something, yet everything looked so different from what I had known before. I insisted on being taken to where my old home had been, but there was no trace of it, or of my old official residence, for both had been destroyed by the Japanese invaders in 1938. I gazed at the stones on the road and the walls of the new houses, and could find no thought or words to describe my feeling. Everything told me that my past had gone forever. "How could this be?" I asked myself, but no answer came. Only the sound of the car moving roused me and I gave my head a violent shake, determined to face the present and future.

Kiukiang, long ago, had good, solid city walls, but as they had ceased to function as protection for the people, I had joined many others in arranging to have such walls pulled down to release more land for housing and also for a wide road around the city. Now the city boundary has extended farther into the countryside because of the need for factory buildings and houses for the workers. During my term of office, from 1930 to the beginning of 1932, the

A young miner enjoying a drink after work, like his counterpart in the West.

only industry was a small textile mill with three hundred or so workers. But
Kuo Chi-fu told me that there were now eighteen good-sized factories producing engineering tools, machine parts, as well as other light industries making
products like fertilizers, matches, and toothpaste. They employed more than
thirty thousand workers, many of whom came from neighboring counties. Everybody in the city had work to do. Kiukiang has become a sort of cosmopolitan place. I like this new development, for all who are born there have a

The author with a few friends sitting in the arbor of the small island of Kan-t'ang Lake,
Kiukiang.

chance to broaden their minds by glimpsing and understanding what goes on
beyond Kiukiang. I remembered how hard I had tried to relieve the poverty
among the people of low income or no income at all, but without success. I
never got help or approval from my superiors in building factories to employ
the poor. The present development in Kiukiang clearly indicates that the
present authorities, from the top to the lower level, work amiably and collectively with one aim, and this had produced the many happy faces that sur-
rounded me now as I visited my home town again.

Presently we drove to the shores of the lake called Kan-t'ang, which had
been an ancient naval training center under the young General Chou Yu of the
Three Kingdoms period. This lake had been my favorite haunt, about which I

wrote much in my book, *A Chinese Childhood,* particularly in the chapter "Boating by Moonlight." Not far from the shore of the lake there was a small island with a little pavilion and an arbor built centuries ago. I used to hire a boat to go over there with friends or relations. Now a stone causeway had been built to join the island to the mainland, so we could walk across. An exhibition of photographs was on at the time, something unheard of in my early days. The pavilion was packed with visitors, young and old. Before only those who had money to hire a boat could enjoy a visit there. Later we went to sit in the arbor and I found my old seat near the edge of the lake. There we rested for a good while. Unwittingly my mind went back to the days when I used to recite old poems or compose my own there. My three companions, Yang, Kuo, and Feng, looked at me smilingly, but none could imagine what was going on in my head. Then Kuo Chi-fu insisted on my having a little rest at a well-known hotel by the lake. When I got there, I exclaimed that this was the place where I had entertained the League of Nations' fact-finding group, led by the English Lord Lytton at the time of the so-called Manchukuo affair in 1931.

I X

Lu Mountain

COMING BACK to Kiukiang after so many years and not going to see my most-beloved Lu Mountain would appear to be utterly absurd. My second son-in-law, born in Peking and married to a girl from Kiukiang, had not yet been up Lu Mountain, so I asked him to come along with me. Yang Shu-tien was born in Pan-pu in Anwei province and had not been up either. So we three, together with Feng Yen-ling, went up Lushan in a car. On our way up I could not help recalling what I had written about my first climb on this mountain in my book *A Chinese Childhood:*

On a warm day in late spring, Father announced that he would take me up Lu Mountain for a few days. Grandmother had no objection. So very early in the morning, we set out. . . .

Our destination was about three thousand feet above us. The highest peak stood at about four thousand feet. The whole mountain was very steep and rocky, but there were good steps forming a path. Father told me that we had plenty of time and need not hurry. We climbed steadily step by step while Father told me stories of the mountain.

Lu Mountain was first inhabited by a man called K'uang Yu, in the later part of Chou, about the fourth century B C. He built the first house on it, and so the mountain was also called K'uang-shan or K'uang Mountain. Since then many well-known people in every dynasty had lived there as hermits. The part called Ku-ling (originally named Cooling by a western missionary) had acquired a snobbish exclusiveness. . . . But the natural beauty spots, he assured me, had not been spoiled by western-style buildings with their red-tiled roofs. . . .

At first we climbed easily through big trees, as if I played hide-and-seek with other climbers, who only appeared now and again in front of us. We came out above the trees and drew away from them until, looking back, they appeared quite small. On the left was the steep slope of the mountain with rocks and trees, on the right a deep valley stretching down the almost vertical slope at my feet, but the view down the valley, the green slope stretching as far as the eye could see, was lovely. . . .

When we reached a small resting arbor, built beside the steps, Father suggested that we should sit down for a while and enjoy the view. . . . We seemed always left behind by those ascending, but Father would not hurry.

At a turn of the path, lifting my head, I saw some people climbing slowly much higher up than ourselves, their tiny figures outlined against the sky. Then I saw three men carrying a sedan-chair.

The step-track we were climbing ran along the edge of the mountain slope and as we rounded shoulders of the mountain I could observe the extraordinary control of the bearers as they mounted the steps. I noticed that the chair shook slightly with the motion, and I thought how courageous the occupant was to ascend so high in a chair. Father said that it was not as dangerous as it looked; the bearers were perfectly at ease and the person riding could admire all the views. After another rest in an arbor we began the last third of the journey. . . .

As it grew dark the evening mists rose. I thought we ought to hurry, but Father smiled and said it would be lovely to climb in the moonlight, when the scene would be beyond description. I was not sorry, for as a matter of fact, I could no longer control my legs. . . . We had dinner at a tiny inn and went early to bed. . . . At five o'clock next morning we stood facing the gap between two mountain slopes, with the wide expanse of the Lake P'o-yang in the far distance. I could not distinguish where the sky ended and the water began. Everything was wrapped in a white shroud tinged with red by the first glow of the rising sun. Later the whole scene became bright red and sparkling. The great ball of fire rose slowly from the water, and diminished as it climbed above the horizon. Father did not speak and I could not express my wonder and excitement. . .

We stayed four days on the mountain. I was taken to as many beautiful spots as there was time to reach:—the Yellow Dragon Fall, the White Dragon Fall, the Black Dragon Fall, the Immortals Cave, the Bridge of Heaven, the Ten-thousand-pine Grove, but unfortunately not to the Three-fold Fall, nor the Five-old-men Peaks.

That was when I was a little more than eleven. Though I have been to Lu Mountain again and again and stayed on it over six months since that time, it had been more than forty-two years since I saw it last. The sensations within me as we made our way up in the car were indescribable, though my companions could not be aware of them. A road had been built in 1952 and there were four bus trips up and down every day, so that all can go up there to enjoy themselves, whereas in the old days it was exclusively for the rich.

We reached Ku-ling where many houses built by the early missionaries now housed mountain workers and those in charge of the mountain amenities. K. P. Chang, of the mountain administration office, came to take us to a hotel for a meal and rest. After that, we went to most of the beauty spots which had been my old haunts. First we saw the Yellow Dragon Falls and the two sacred old trees which were said to have been planted there in the fourth century. Chinese botanists have made a study of these two sacred trees and thought they were about eight hundred years old. They are tall and still full of lively new growth on the top branches. I could not tell what kinds they were. They did not resemble the *Sequoia sempervirens,* or California redwood, nor the dawn redwood, or *Metasequoia,* of China; both are trees which can live to a very old age. I had had an exhibition of my paintings in Yellow Dragon Monastery here in 1931; the old monastery had been destroyed by lightning some years later.

Next the Black Dragon Falls detained us for a good while, as beautiful as they had ever been. A young boy was swimming in the pool below the falls and did

Black Dragon Falls, Lushan, Kiukiang.

not seem to mind the cold water. We went on to Han-p'o-kou, facing the gap between two mountain slopes with the wide expanse of Lake P'o-yang in the far distance. This was where I had watched the sunrise with my father more than sixty years ago. My father's love for me and his training to make me a painter filled my heart with poignant feeling. I grieved that he was no longer here to join his long-wandering son who had come back to see his beloved mountain. Death has been treated by the philosophers of many countries as a shadow in the journey of life, but why should trees continue to live and not men?

From Han-p'o-kou we came to the Immortals' Cave where a new structure with a moon gate had been added at the entrance. Many visitors were there already, occupying the benches and taking cold drinks and cakes. Another small building had been put up close by to house a gilded-clay figure of Lao Tzu, the recognized originator of Chinese Taoism. I particularly wanted to see the statue inside. It turned out to be a figure of an old man leaning on a buffalo stretched out at his side. This looked odd to me, for if all the old Chinese books were right,

Fishing with a net on Lake P'o-yang, Kiangsi.

Lao Tzu rode through the Han-ku Pass to the west on the back of an ox, not a buffalo. No buffaloes were employed for ploughing fields in north China. I made a quick sketch of the clay figure. Walking down from the cave we saw many striking rock formations, one of which, sticking out of the precipitous cliff, had four Chinese Characters engraved on it: 縱覽雲飛, *Tsung-lan-yun-fei,* or "Boundless view of flying clouds." This was a favorite beauty spot where one could walk near the edge and be photographed by a professional photographer. We waited for a chance to go to the edge ourselves. We also went up to the memorial commemorating the rescue by the monk Chou Tien-hsien of Chu Hung-wu, the first emperor of the Ming dynasty, when he was pursued by his enemies right up the mountainside.

Yu-pei-ting, a memorial arbor built to commemorate the rescue of the first emperor of the Ming dynasty by Chou Tien-hsien, on Lushan, Kiukiang.

Later we climbed up to the top of another beauty spot, Hsiao-tien chih, for a grand view of the spacious valley below, which stretched far away to the city of Kiukiang. Nearby this spot was a noted botanic garden, not in existence during my term of office. Since 1962 it had been under the able direction of Dr. W. C. Chen; he had recently been transferred to work in Kwangtung. Now the director is Mu Tsung-shan. It contained thousands of plants chiefly grown on Lu Mountain. But I had a talk with the resident research worker about the Western botanists who had been collecting plants from China since 1843. Though I am no botanist or gardener, I became interested in learning more about Chinese plants during my stay in England from 1933 to 1954, for many of my English friends were good gardeners and owned big gardens themselves. In their libraries I read much about Chinese plants. One of the most interesting books was *China, Mother of Gardens* by Ernest H. Wilson, keeper of the Arnold Aboretum of Harvard University, in which he wrote,

> China is, indeed, the Mother of Gardens, for of the countries to which our gardens are most deeply indebted she holds the foremost place. From the bursting into blossom of the forsythia and Yulan magnolia in the early spring to the peonies and roses in summer and the chrysanthemums in the autumn. To China the flower lover owes the parents of the modern rose, be they tea or hybrid tea, rambler or polyantha; likewise his greenhouse azaleas and primroses, and the fruit grower, his peaches, oranges, lemons and grapefruits. It is safe to say that there is no garden in this country or in Europe that is without its Chinese representatives and these rank among the finest of trees, shrub, herb and vine.

Wilson came to collect plants in China from 1899 to 1911. He was based in Szechwan, but he passed through Kiukiang many a time and must have been up Lu Mountain to find plants there.

I told the research worker in the botanic garden about the Portuguese who reached China by sea in 1516 and took back with them to their settlement in India the sweet orange, which later was introduced into Portugal, and from there went to the new world of the Americas. That is how the United States came to be so famous for its oranges and other citrus fruits, all of which have their origins in China. I also told him what I had read about Charles Marias. In 1879 he went up the Yangtze River as far as I-ch'ang where he collected *Primula obconica;* he then stopped off and gathered seeds of *Loropetalum Chinense* and its relative *Hamamelis mollis,* finest of all the witch hazels. They were all surprised to know this; they had no witch hazel in their collection.

Lu mountain has been well-known to Chinese painters and poets since the fourth century, but the Western botanists know about it only on account of its rare and beautiful plants. However, a friend of mine, Professor R. A. Davis of the Department of Oriental Studies at the University of Sydney, Australia, who specialized in Chinese literature and did a good many translations of Chinese classical poetry from the early Chin dynasty to the late T'ang period, particularly asked to be taken up Lu Mountain when he visited China in 1965. He wanted to find the ancient hut where the great poet Tao Yuan-ming had lived in the fourth century. He was fortunate enough to do so, but I had no time to look for it.

Next morning I suggested going to see the famous Five-old-men Peak on the south side of the mountain. My companions thought I wanted to climb it, but in fact I did not. K. P. Chang said we should have a good view of it on our way back to the city in the afternoon. So we moved on to the Shih-men-kan Falls instead. We walked along a narrow footpath with luxuriant growth on both sides. Eventually we emerged into a good-sized tea plantation, which I was told produced the *yun-wu-cha,* or ''cloud-and-mist tea,'' now exported all over China and abroad too. In the old days this kind of tea used to be planted in the small back yard of an ancient monastery. The new, young leaves would be picked by the monks and dried in the sun, then brewed to entertain occasional visitors. It was not for sale then. This tea has a clean, refreshing flavor particularly good if it is made with the water from a mountain spring. Now it is grown as a special local product and I saw many young people set up to help cultivate it. This means that Lu Mountain now is not only a beauty spot for artists and poets but also has a commercial function.

From the tea plantation we continued on a little further toward the famous waterfall. To my great surprise there were no falls here, only a tiny trickle of water coming down through the thickets. The big painting of this spot, called ''Lu-shan-kao,'' by Shen Chou (1427–1509) is well-known. How could the great waterfall have dwindled to almost nothing in five hundred or so years? A stone bridge was still there as I remembered it. We sat down for a rest beside the path, not far from the bridge. An old peasant came to talk to us, asking if we would like to have some tea. A most welcome offer, but there was no time to wait for the water to be boiled. It was a very sunny, clear, and warm day, a rare occurrence, for Lu Mountain is known to be often lost in clouds, as described in the famous line by the Sung poet Su Tung-po: ''I cannot recognize the real face of Lushan. For I have been engulfed in it,'' 不識盧山眞面目，祇緣身在此山中.

After breakfast the next morning, K. P. Chang came to tell me that we were driving back to the city and would have many splendid views on the way down. Again we had a fine day, sunny though not too warm. From the newly built road we had one splendid panorama after another as the car turned round curve upon curve. I never before had the chance to see Lu Mountain this way, covering much of the full face in a few short hours, though wandering there on foot had its own pleasures too. We stopped at a building which formerly had been a monastery but was now a school for youngsters from the local commune. Standing by the porch and looking far into the distance, I caught sight of 雙劍峰, Shuang-chien-feng, or *''Twin-Rapier Peak.''* Near to it, a long, silk-ribbon-like waterfall hung down beautifully. I lingered for a good while before returning to the car. Another beauty spot called 漱玉泉, Sou-yu-chuan, or ''Rinsing-Jade Falls,'' took no time to reach. Walking through some thick undergrowth, we came to sit in the newly painted and repaired Sou-yu-ting, or "Rinsing-Jade Arbor." Near the roof a long poem about this particular waterfall by Su Tung-po was engraved on one of the long stone beams. I enjoyed reading it. Then we moved on to look for the source of the bubbling and rushing sound and to our delight we reached the spot where the waterfall was coiling down over the rocky surface of a hill between two precipitous cliffs. The sun was shining directly on it, making the falls look like a group of soft silvery ropes. An unforgettable sight.

We were now at the foot of the mountain in the county of Hsing-tzu. Peasants, men and women, were busy in the fields, for the end of May and the beginning of June is the vital time for weeding and separating the rice plants. Everything in

Working in the rice fields.

sight was in different shades of green, except the mountain slopes which now looked bluish from the distance. A special convalescent center came into sight. It had been built beside a famous hot spring discovered centuries ago. The waters here were especially valuable for their medicinal qualities, for curing skin diseases and other complaints. We were invited to have a hot-spring bath, and I certainly felt deliciously refreshed afterward. The superintendent of the center came to tell us some part of the history of the place. It had been in a state of delapidation when he came to take it over in 1951, for the Japanese soldiers had done inestimable damage. It took months to get it working again. Now five people were in residence and more were coming. As this center is not near any big city, the patients must have a special recommendation from their doctors or from the local authorities.

The Five-old-men Peak was pointed out to me on the opposite side of Lushan soon after we left the center. The car went on slowly and then stopped for a moment to let me glance over the whole range. This peak seemed like an enormous rice bowl turned upside down with its uneven base of many knobby shapes facing upward to the sky. These knobs were the five old men, though there seemed to be more than five; the smaller ones might be their attendants. This peak is highly paintable, a marvelous work of the Creator, impossible to describe

Five-old-men Peak from the distance, Lushan, Kiukiang.

in words. So beautiful it is, towering and majestic, no wonder it has been so beloved by painters and poets. Li Po of the T'ang dynasty wrote of it,

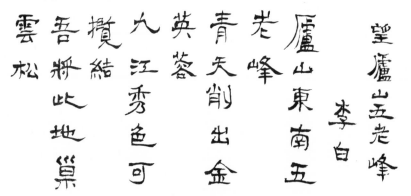

望廬山五老峰

李白

廬山東南五
老峰
青天削出金
英蓉
九江秀色可
攬結
吾將此地巢
雲松

On the southeast of Lu Mountain the Five-old-men Peak,
Like a golden lotus carved against the blue sky.
The beautiful scenery of Kiukiang seen all in one glance;
I shall come to live here among the cloudy pines.

All sorts of trees, but particularly pines, grow upon the slopes of this peak and on the lower hills in front of it as well. The upper part of the peak, quite rocky and rugged, is highly suitable for Chinese brushwork. Its circumference is huge and its summit now looked unattainable from the road. I was glad to have seen it so clearly, as if someone had dispersed the clouds and mists for me on purpose. But I was not disputing Su Tung-po's comment that constant clouds and mist often covered parts of the mountain, for this had been my own experience in the past. The three sunny days high up on Lu Mountain on this trip of mine were really a special treat.

Both Li Po and Su Tung-po wrote about the beauty spots of Lu Mountain from the south side and it seemed to me that since early T'ang days people must have come to see Lu Mountain from the southern part not from the north side as we did.

We reached the city of Kiukiang about four o'clock and went to have a wash and rest. In the evening a sumptuous dinner was given in my honor by the local administration office, headed by Han Yun-cheng and Kuo Chi-fu, for I was a native son who had come to see his birthplace after almost half a century of wandering abroad. The usual custom at a Chinese banquet is for the host to drink his guest's health by *kan-pei* or "bottoms up," which the guest should return with another *kan-pei,* and this would go on, one after another, until the guest became really giddy and confused in speech. I knew it

An old fisherman seeing to his net.

only too well, yet it seemed hopeless to keep telling my host and other guests that I was no drinker, particularly since today's fashionable Chinese drink, *Mao-tai,* was in good supply on another table nearby. They had previously discovered that I was fond of fresh-water fish, so the entire set of courses consisted of fish in one form or another. The dinner was called a fish banquet, like the duck banquet I had in Peking. It had been specially prepared by three young cooks who were called up to join us for a drink. I was landed in a terrible position, for I had to return their kindness by drinking three more cups. I could not talk too well by then, but they all laughed, having no idea of what I was talking about. It was a joyous and unprecedented evening in my life.

After dinner I went with the rest to see a show given by the Kangwu-chü elementary school which had won a reputation as one of the best theatrical teams in a nationwide contest a year or so before. Hundreds of young school children, none older than twelve, were taking part or had come as spectators. The first item was clearly announced by a girl of six, and then a number of young girls and boys, from four to ten years of age, came to the front of the stage, to dance, play, and sing. They had been well trained and none of them made any false steps. Several other items followed: a Western orchestra, music with Chinese instruments, a brief comic play, a fighting scene, and so on. Then came a solo violin player, a little girl of four, not as tall as the top bar of her chair. After a slight bow she began to play the violin like a professional without any sign of nervousness or fidgeting. I am no musician, either in the Chinese or Western style, but I admired her self-control and poise at such a tender age. She had helped her school, I was told, to win a first award among all the other schools. Afterward I went up to the stage to shake hands with her and she was not a bit shy and even curtsied to me, perfectly at ease. Most of the songs, dances, and music had become familiar to me, for I had seen similar shows in other places, but to see them all performed in my native city had a special meaning for me.

Kangwu-chü is the local bureau in charge of Kiukiang harbor affairs. The harbor of Kiukiang has long been an important outlet for products from the whole of Kiangsi Province as well as from neighboring provinces, whence they can be transported to other parts of China and even abroad, for it is on the middle course of the Yangtze River. It is because it was so important that Kiukiang became one of the five treaty ports, and a foreign concession was created there, occupying a good part of the wharves. English steamboats and those of other countries could sail inland from Shanghai right up to Hankow, passing through Kiukiang. Now no foreign establishment existed here. I noticed the dock area had been extended with more wharves for local boats to load and unload goods, far different from what it was in my days. The riverside was full of workers and it looked very prosperous. The bureau is run by a committee whose members are elected by old and new workers. With so

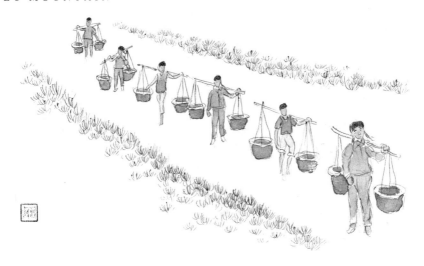

Carrying products to the city.

many new activities and a bigger harbor population there would be more children to attend the school established and run by the bureau. They employed good teachers and all worked together with a collective spirit to bring up the young people well, so they in turn would do good for the country when they grew up. The show which their young students put on was a testimonial to their efforts. I composed the following little verse and wrote it in my own style of calligraphy to send to the school:

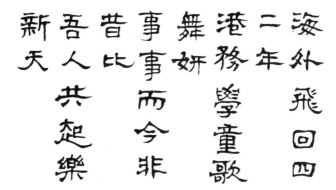

Returning home after forty-two years,
I enjoy the dancing and singing of the Kan-wu-chü's children.
Everything is different now, not to be compared with old times;
We all gather together and rejoice under a new Heaven.

Next day I returned to Nan-ch'ang for another fitting of my new teeth at the Provincial Hospital there and found there would be another three days to wait for the completion. After having spent hours with my wife and children, I asked Yang Shu-tien and Tao Lo-li to go with me for a look at Chiangkang-shan, the old headquarters of the Chinese Red Army some fifty years ago. We left Nan-chang in the morning and reached Hsin-kan county in time for lunch. We were in Chi-an County for tea and then, crossing the newly built modern bridge over the Kan River, we arrived at Tzu-p'ing Center, where we stayed in a hotel.

I had never traveled this inland way before and was glad to have a good look at the green fields and well-cultivated slopes of the mountains and hills all the way. Tzu-p'ing is in the middle of the Chingkangshan Mountains, quite high up, three thousand or more feet above sea level, and is situated near the border of Hunan Province where Chairman Mao Tse-tung was born.

Before the 1920s, people seldom traveled to see this mountain area, for it contains no beautiful waterfalls or any other beauty spots to have attracted poets and painters. It was not known to most people of China. It only became historic after Chairman Mao led the Autumn Harvest Uprising at Sanwan in 1927 and carried out a troop reorganization, moving to Lingkan and then to Ta-ching, inside the huge mountain range of Chingkangshan. There was some level ground at Tzu-p'ing with a few farm houses, so it was chosen as the center for the Red Army. Another revolutionary force led by Marshal Chu

Two old trees high up in the Chingkangshan Mountains where Marshal Chu Teh and Mao Tse-tung met to reorganize the Red Army.

Teh came to meet Chairman Mao here and it soon became known as the first headquarters of the Chinese Red Army. As this is a natural fortress with clusters of sloping ranges full of rocks, crags and gullies, it is difficult to penetrate. The upper heights are densely wooded and the thick growth continues right down the lower slope to the base of the mountains. The villagers living in that handful of houses handed down from their forefathers were all very poor, trying to produce whatever they could get out of the land; they had no knowledge of what was going on in the world outside.

When the first Red base was created at Chingkangshan they had endless difficulties with food and shelter. By and by they made plans, the soldiers and the local peasants received explanations and education, and they began to work together to cultivate the fields to grow more food and they constructed more houses. They had actually transformed the mountainous area into a habitable quarter. The Chingkangshan base was a critical test for the later achievements and success. By October 1934, many corps of the Red Army started their Long March for thousands of miles through treacherous country and eventually reached the Shensi-Kansu base on October 20, 1935. Later Yenan became the second headquarters, where much more planning and education were carried out before the final victory. But this first base at Chingkangshan had its particular interest in the history of China during the present century. It made me realize that no matter how hard and difficult a situation might be, solid determination to do good for the people would eventually overcome every obstacle.

When we woke up the next morning, it was still pouring heavily after a whole night of rain. It was difficult to walk about at first. After lunch we went to see the house where Chairman Mao had lived for a few years and

Mao Tse-tung's living quarters in the Chingkangshan Mountains.

"Rain and clouds have been busy high on Chingkangshan."

also two rocks nearby where he used to sit, read, and think out the next steps to be taken in the campaign. A large tree, called locally *tung-shu,* was pointed out to me as the first meeting place of Mao Tse-tung and Chu Teh for the reorganization of the Red Army. Huang Yang Chieh Pass, one of the five passes into the mountain base, is about forty-four hundred feet above sea level. In 1928, Chiang Kai-shek ordered the Nationalist Army to penetrate the pass, but they failed. Chairman Mao wrote a Poem about the pass in the autumn of that year:

At the mountain foot our banners,
On the mountain crest sound bugles and drums,
The foe round us in their thousands.
We stood fast, unmoving.

Our defense a stout wall about us,
Now our wills unite, impregnable fortress.
From Huang Yang Chieh the thunder of guns,
The enemy fades at night.*

Another big tree was said to have been a resting place when Chairman Mao used to help carry grain up to the houses on the hill. The old barracks and the hospital at Hsiao-ching as well as a few memorial monuments were all shown to us.

The whole area has now become a handsome country town on the hill with many working units around it. I talked to a few young people who acted as guides as well as doing other types of work. To my surprise they told me that they all came from the Shanghai area, about two thousand of them. In the old days very few Shanghai people came as far as the Kiangsi provincial capital, Nan-ch'ang, let alone further inland into the mountainous area to work. They said that when they graduated from high school they were asked to choose from a list of places where they would like to work. These two thousand, all

* Translated by Han Suyin.

around twenty years of age, decided to work in Chingkangshan. I asked if
they were ever homesick for Shanghai, a great city where life was far different from the country life here in the mountains. They all explained happily
that they had a month's home leave each year with expenses paid.

A memorial for the dead of the Red Army in the Chingkangshan Mountains.

I discovered another hopeful development. Chingkangshan has an abundant
growth of trees and shrubs which had never been used before. A few years
ago a factory for bamboo and woodwork was set up. I went specially to see it
and found everyone working at high pressure. The man in charge of the factory, Ma Kuang-chih, told me that they were all doing overtime because a big
order had come from Italy for their small boxes covered with the inside-skin
of the bamboo. This was a change indeed that an order should come from
Italy for this special Kiangsi product. The development of local products in
this way is a good sign of the stability of China's economy. Tzu-p'ing, an unknown place before, has the prospect of becoming a small cosmopolitan
center in the middle of China. People from all over the country have come
and will come to pay their homage to the headquarters where the new China
was created. The heavy rain and masses of white clouds moving over the
mountain slopes blotting out the land, made me feel that we were in a completely new world.

On our way down the mountain for the return journey, the sky suddenly
cleared up and I had never seen a greener environment; it was as if everything
had been washed all at once. The flying clouds were trying to race with the
speedy movement of our car.

雲 井 聖 海 南 全 能 江
忙 崗 地 外 昌 家 忘 西
　 山 　 飛 大 　 　 使
　 上 　 來 小 　 　 我
　 雨 　 参 集 　 　 不

Kiangsi gives me unforgettable memories:
All my kinsfolk have gathered in Nan-ch'ang.
I flew from overseas to visit this Sacred Land;
Rain and clouds have been busy high on Chingkangshan.

The above little verse I composed on the way before reaching my daughter's home. As this would be the last evening I should spend with all my kinsfolk, my head was full of thoughts again on entering the gate.

I have moved about from place to place throughout a large portion of the world; nowhere had caused me so much pain in parting as I felt in leaving Nan-ch'ang on my way to New York again. It was no good for me to say that I did not want to leave, for many reasons would not let me stay on. The dinner I had with my kinsfolk then became a sorrowful one for all, mixed with occasional smiles. The thought of parting can be even more unbearable than actual parting.

Before leaving I had to go to the hospital for a final check on my new teeth. I actually asked to have two sets made and one of them I wore on my trip to Chingkangshan. All the doctors of the hospital received me as courteously as before. I told them that I had had no trouble and that the set was well made. Eventually came the charge for the two sets I had asked for— thirty Chinese dollars for each set which was two or three hundred times less than I would have had to pay in New York. It was incredible. But the doctors said that this was the usual charge. I could not find adequate words to express my gratitude for having saved me so much money. All these doctors have become my new friends in China. I told them that many of my American doctor friends would feel surprise and admiration that my new teeth were so good and comfortable.

My two daughters and their husbands decided to see me off at Canton for my return trip to America via Hong Kong. They behaved quite calmly, but the five young grandchildren were very upset. I could judge their feelings from my own. I particularly did not want to leave my wife again, for we are growing old; but she seemed to be quite resigned, for she could not walk even a step. I could only lay the blame for our sadness on the past rulers of China who had brought so much suffering on their people including me, by causing the breakup of my family. The five youngsters had not known their grandfather until now and my short stay had created a firm attachment between us. They did not want me to go back, though they understood the situation quite well. Their faces grew red and I forced myself to smile at them, saying that I would try to come back again soon. They begged to go along with me in the train for a few more small stations. When the last station was reached and they had to return home while I changed to another train going direct to Canton, the tears began to fall. The three younger girls hid their faces and could not even look up to wave goodby, and the elder girl kept running with the train. It was a deeply touching moment for me, an old man in my seventies.

At Canton I had another trip to make before returning to the United States. I was to fly to Kuei-lin. Kuei-lin had been famous for more than a thousand years for its unusual natural scenery of hills and water. It is situated in the southwest of China's Kwangsi Chuang Autonomous Region. As its scenery had been so well described in many poems since the T'ang and Sung periods, of the seventh to the thirteenth centuries, I, like thousands of Chinese youngsters who read those poems, had longed to visit it in my young days but never had had the opportunity, for it was so far away from my home city. I therefore grasped this chance and asked to have at least two days reserved for the trip.

Kuei-lin and Yang-shuo

YANG SHU-TIEN and I boarded the plane after our arrival in Canton and reached Kuei-lin in the afternoon about three o'clock. Ho Li-chih, from the local China Travel Service, took us to the Kuei-lin Hotel, passing on the way an old wall said to be part of a mansion erected for a prince of the T'ang period. Not far from the old wall, a large, flourishing banyan tree had been left in the middle of the road. Kuei-lin has a subtropical climate and in the early summer everywhere is filled with green trees and red blossoms. There was a nice courtyard attached to the hotel. After a good meal, we walked in the garden and then had a stroll along the banks of the Yunghu, or Banyan Lake, named after a tree that used to be a landmark in the city but which had died long ago.

Later Ho Li-chih arranged for a car to take us to see Tieh-tsai-shan, or Hill with Piled-up-Colors, a name leading one to expect something brilliant. Going through a natural stone gate we found some good Buddhist carvings on the rocky cliffs, evidently of the T'ang period. Professor Lo Hsiang-lin of Hong Kong University had written about this in his book *T'ang Tai Kuei-lin chih Mo-yai Fu Hsiang* (Tang dynasty cliff carvings of Buddha images at Kuei-lin). Unfortunately there was no time for me to make a careful study of the carvings; they had obvious artistic merit and historic value. As they were in a rather obscure place, they had escaped damage by robbers and also had been saved from being taken to some Western museum, like those from the Yunkang caves.

There was a small stream, clear down to the bottom, running over the rocks. A big hole in the rock led up to the top of the cliff where there were stone benches for visitors to sit and gaze around. It was an incredible sight that stretched out before us. Numerous steep hills rose straight out of the plain, while red-roofed and whitewashed houses and streets zigzagged down below and around them. This was the city of Kuei-lin. I had never seen a sight like this with straight, vertical-sided hills right among houses inside and outside a city. The steep hills looked like a number of giants guarding the city closely and well. I walked on up a stone path toward an even higher rocky cliff and was confronted with a most memorable and amazing view of mountain peaks, one layer of mountains piled up behind another, and yet another, and so on. This was the lofty landscape of the early Chinese painters' works of T'ang and Sung periods. It was almost unbelievable to see such a landscape in reality and so near at hand. In one glance over

Cormorant fishing in Kuei-lin, Kwangsi.

the whole scene one could see hundreds and thousands of such upright steep hills scattered over the plain. Though I have traveled on five continents and across seven seas in the past forty-odd years, I could not say that I had seen anything like this. The Bryce Canyon, King's Canyon, and Zion Canyon in the west of North America are formed of dry, red or brown rocks with little or nothing growing on them—barren landscapes. But every steep hill in Kuei-lin was thickly covered with trees and shrubs growing among the piled white limestone. They looked like living columns of emerald rising from the ground from time immemorial.

Afterward Ho Li-chih took us to see the Lo-to-shan, or Camellike Hill, and the Hsiang-pi-shan, or Elephant's Trunk Hill, both named for their shapes. We also had a look at the Ch'i-hsing-yai, or Cliffs of the Seven Stars, which was a formation of seven steep hills linked to one another. A tradition said that they were originally seven big stars which had fallen together from the sky on this spot.

Not far from our hotel was the famous Kuei-lin landmark, the Hua-chiao, or Flower Bridge, originally built by a local governor, Ho Yung-chuan in 1443; it had been rebuilt and repaired again and again. This bridge with a roof over it, similar to the New England covered bridges of America, became known in Chinese art through a painting of it by the late Kao Chi-feng done at the beginning of this century.

Apart from many others dotted around, a specially conspicuous steep hill within the city of Kuei-lin, called Tu-hsiu-feng, or the Peak of Solitary Charm, rose five hundred feet straight up from the ground, with no other mound or hill at its foot. Standing as it does in the center of the city, it attracts anyone coming to see Kuei-lin. Yang Shu-tien and I were no exception. We followed Ho Li-chih and climbed it without hesitation.

There were 360 rocky steps winding upward, bordered by a low stone wall. A small pavilion with curved roof was built on the summit, and there we sat down for a rest and gazed about at all the other steep hills, like masses of bamboo shoots springing up. A narrow river around the city flowed like a long, winding, silvery silk ribbon as if it were tying the city into a large parcel. I have read many old poems written about this Peak of Solitary Charm, but the following one expressed my feeling at the time:

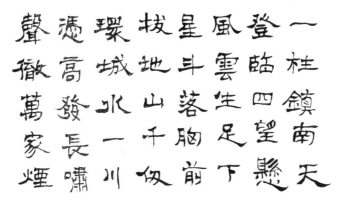

It stands like a pillar to guard the southern sky,
I climbed up and gazed in all directions.
Wind and clouds rise from beneath my feet.
Stars and constellations fall before my breast.
Straight up from the earth this hill of hundreds of feet,
Surrounding the whole city the waters of River Li.
Having climbed so high I breathe a long relaxing sigh.
Its sound stirs the smoke from thousands of chimneys!

The author of this poem is unknown. Some lights down below looked like stars upside down while the real stars above became dim. On the way down the steps, these upside-down stars seemed to be alive, playing hide and seek with me behind the trees. The evening mist, though very thin at first, rose steadily and was about to veil the city, clothing it with a tantalizing beauty. I felt well satisfied with my first sight of Kuei-lin and went to bed for a sound sleep.

After breakfast the next day, Ho Li-chih came to invite Yang Shu-tien and me to the Li River for a boat trip to another county, Yang-shuo. I thought we might be going on a small old-fashioned Chinese rowboat or punt or a bamboo raft, quite close to the shore, right underneath the steep rocky hills. Ho-

Li-chih broke into a broad smile, saying that it would take several days for us to reach our destination that way. Instead, we were told to jump onto a big junklike boat with many other visitors from another group. A small steamer then towed us along the middle of the stream. Twenty or more of us were packed on the decks, but I managed to find a space from which to watch the trooplike, pinnacle-shaped hills passing one after another. After some time, the river bed became wider. As our boat remained in the middle of the stream, I got a more distant view of the whole landscape facing our boat. A faint mist veiling one part or another made the scene look real yet not real. The water near the shore was shallow and a few bamboo rafts were punted slowly by, looking from a distance as if the punters were walking on the water. I was told that there were more than three hundred shallow rapids along the whole course of the Li River and that those boatmen had to be well experienced, otherwise there might be some disasters.

The river then became even wider than before and the steep hills along the banks looked like some carved green chess pieces making moves in one direction or another while our boat glided by. At places there was a wide embankment with rice fields and some little village houses with bamboo growing thickly behind or beside them. However, these bamboo seemed to be a different kind from those varieties I knew in the Yangtze River valley; they had long, thin stems with leaves right up to the tips; they bend and sway in the wind like long phoenix tails—hence their name, *Feng-wei-chu,* or Phoenix-tail bamboo.

After another twenty minutes or so our boat reached a point from which we could see the well-known Hua-shan, or Painted Hill, a hill with a whitish precipitous surface and various rocky markings that seemed from a distance to represent a painting of horses. After that, a new panorama opened out. Someone shouted that we had reached Hsing-ping. This reminded me at once of a poem written by General Yeh Chien-ying, the minister of defense, which I roughly translate:

詠灘江

葉劍英

春風灘水客舟輕

夾岈奇峰相送迹

馬跃画山人隔境

果然佳景在興坪

> Spring wind on River Li, I in my light boat,
> Fantastic peaks on both banks welcome and escort me.
> The horses galloping on the "painted cliff" are far away,
> Indeed, the best beauty spot is at Hsing-ping.

Just as our boat began to pass this famous spot, by a most untimely arrangement, we were summoned to lunch. All the passengers gathered together in
the center of the boat talking and eating. I had to come down from the upper
deck to join them. I deeply regretted having to miss seeing Hsing-ping, a very
old town built by the ruler of the Wu Kingdom in the Three Kingdoms period
of the third century.

The weather was mild with no wind and the sensation of gliding along on
the crystal-clear water with those fantastic steep hills on either side was sheer
joy. Gradually the faint image of a city appeared in the distance on our left.
Here the shapes of the steep hills began to look rather different. Some looked
rounder in shape and sometimes two or three joined together. This was the
county of Yang-shuo that we had come to see. The respective beauties of
Kuei-lin and Yang-shuo have been debated by visitors over the centuries,
some extolling one and some the other.

While we approached our destination, one of the passengers began to describe to me a local legend about three of the hills we were passing—Yu-nu-
shan, or Jade Maiden hill; Tung-lan-shan, or Eastern Youth hill, and Hsi-
lan-shan, or Western Youth hill. Thousands of years ago, the jade maiden
loved boths boys dearly, but she had to choose between them. One day she
saw both approaching her in a rush at the same time. Quickly she took off her
jade hairpin and scratched a line on the earth which immediately cracked and
became the Li River. But even before the transformation could take place, the
western youth jumped over the line and came to the jade maiden. So they later
married, while the eastern boy remained on the opposite bank till the present
day. This is a kind of legend I have heard before in Japan and Southeast Asia
about hills and mountains, though never in Europe and America.

Faintly but clearly I saw a stone wall underneath a huge cluster of weeping
willow leaves by the shore. Our boat had been unloosed from the small
steamer which drew us up here; one or two boatmen maneuvered the boat into
an anchorage by the bank, then we all walked down the gangway. There were
a good many young people, boys and girls in bright dresses with flowers on
their heads, climbing on the wall or standing by the roadside to watch us. A
number of cars were lined up on the road to take their respective visitors. Ho
Li-chih led us to ours. There was no time for us to have a stroll about in the
city of Yang-shuo. Around the suburbs and further into the countryside of the
county more and more of those fantastically shaped steep hills loomed up
singly and in groups here and there. At places a few of them sprung right up

among the rice fields and the view of them from a distance was most dramatic and spectacular. Our car drove between them and we got out to stand right in front of the hills for a closer look at various angles. My hands were itching all the way and I wanted to paint on the spot, in this place and that. Time was so short there but memories will linger. I returned to the hotel and, lying down to rest, remembered the sights with much delight, but it was mixed with regret for the flying visit. I hope I shall come to see Kuei-lin and Yang-shuo again one day.

Before I visited these places I was inclined to think those steep hills had been formed by lava erupted from ancient volcanoes millions of year ago, as were the Glasshouse Mountains in East Australia. But, on careful examination, I found each steep hill was made up of white and gray limestone blocks, not black lava, and each had caves hollowed out where one could walk around. Being no student of geology, I wrote to ask my good friend, Dr. N. J. Jennings, a noted geomorphologist at the Australian National University, Canberra, about it, for he had been invited to visit this county with five other scientists, all with a particular interest in the Quaternary period (the last couple of million years of geological time), by the Chinese Academy of Sciences in Peking. Dr. Jennings answered,

> One could write a great deal about the country you ask about, what we call tower karst. . . . The usual explanation of the towers of limestone (which of course feature in so many forms of Chinese art and seem incredible to Western eyes) is that it represents an advanced state of solutional sculpture of pure limestone in a hot, humid climate given a fair amount of geological time for solution to have proceeded without much interference. . . . We could not escape getting impressed by what is probably the finest and largest karst area in the world.

Again, he wrote,

> In the Kuei-lin and Yang-shuo region, the geology consists of a faulted N-S trending synclinal basin, followed by the Li River which is thus a longitudinal river. Middle and Upper Devonian rocks prevail together with some Upper Carboniferous beds. Seventy per cent of the rock thickness and ninety-eight per cent of the area are formed of the carbonate rocks. These are mostly limestones, which weather to a gray color, with some dolomites which take on a darker hue. There are four terrace systems along the Li River, the highest of which, forty meters above it, is regarded as glaciofluvial and of Middle Pleistocene age. The pronounced tectonic disturbances promoted ground water circulation and so also the development of elaborate karst topography. Successive uplifts since the Mesozoin have led to multiple stories in the karst relief, with a corresponding development of caves at several levels in the carbonate residue.

Karst is, I was then told, the name of a place in east Yugoslavia where the land is formed of limestone. Thus *karst* is used by the geologists for any

"Both Kuei-lin and Yang-shuo glorify our divine land."

place formed of limestone. Most of Dr. Jennings's expressions were beyond my understanding, but the so-called karst area remains in my mind as a most paintable subject. With these beautiful natural formations, Chinese artists of the past centuries as well as many of the present century have been greatly blessed by the rich endowment from nature to which they were born. Great art is indeed purely a man's creation, but it needs the support and help of the heavenly creator.

Dr. Jennings told me that he and his group of Australian scientists had managed to see many places such as Ch'ang-chia-k'ou, Choukoutien, Yenan, Kweiyang, the important Liukiang-man cave near Liu-chou, the Seven Stars Crags near Chaoching. They also visited many research institutes in various places and a palaeomagnetic laboratory, where they met their Chinese counterparts and both sides gave lectures in turn—all in three weeks' time. Dr. Jennings concluded his impressions of the short visit by saying, "We must look forward to more interchange with Chinese cave and karst scientists, because there is so very much interest in China for outside speleologists." When he thanked the Chinese in charge of the arrangements for the excellent treatment of his group, he received the answer, "Scientists are much more important than politicians in China." Dr. Jennings was most touched and impressed by these few words. So was I, when I heard them. The comment took me back to my days in China before 1933, when scientific study was in its infancy and there were no good laboratories to speak of. How had the new government in Peking been able to produce so many scientists in different subjects and also to establish so many research institutes all over China? It was an unbelievable achievement. In scientific studies China is no longer backward!

Kuei-lin has been famous for its beauty since it was founded during the Han dynasty, about 206 B.C. It has long been an attractive place for artists and men of letters; it seems now a center for foreign visitors. After lunch, Ho Li-chih came to the hotel again to take Yang Shu-tien and me to a most characteristic cave called Lu-ti-yai, or Reedflute Cavern, which lies a few kilometers south of the city of Kuei-lin. It has been known in history as far back as the T'ang dynasty. But after the end of the Sung dynasty, wars and disturbances transformed it into a refuge for the ordinary people in the area. It was not until 1959 that the beauties of this mysterious cavern were rediscovered. After more than ten years of reconstruction, it has now become known far and wide and is visited by thousands yearly. Workers cleared away, by hand, thousands of tons of small stones under the close supervision of experts so that no damage was caused to the natural formations. The cave is well above plain level, within a large residual peak. Inside, a single large room stretches about 820 feet long and 260 feet wide. Its ceiling is 50 feet high. There are many decorations and strange forms; some parts were wet, but there was practically no dripping. Many tall stalactites, both bulky and slender can be seen clearly and a number of pillars reach the roof, without interfering with the spaciousness of the cave. Most of the inside of the cave is reddish in color, but colorful lights brought out various other shades dazzling to the eyes. I remembered a poem by Wang Li, the well-known philologist, which described this cavern very aptly:

喜從地下得天宮
洞府幽深曲徑通
玉柱雕楹資鬼斧
碧文圓頂是神工
天教名勝裝新國
地以靈奇餉健翁
出洞莫嗟人境熱
披襟猶可招雄風

蘆笛岩

王力

I rejoice to find a Heavenly Palace beneath the earth,
This cavern, deep and quiet, is reached by a twisted path.
The jadelike pillars and carved walls could have been shaped by a mystic ax;
The green designs on its domed ceiling are the work of spirits.
Heaven bids this famous cave adorn our new nation,
Earth provides wonder for a strong man to enjoy.
We need not complain of the heat in the human world when we emerge:
We should unbutton our coats to receive a healthy wind!

There were several hours yet before we went to catch our plane back to Canton. I sat by the window on the second floor of the hotel, gazing at the steep hills behind the city of Kuei-lin. It was very satisfying for me that I had come to see this famous karst area at long last. But besides the lovely scenery, I had learned something else about the place: It was the life of the local people, those born, bred, and who have lived here for centuries which had puzzled me, for not much had been written about them in the long history of China. Kuei-lin was first included in the territory of China in 221 B.C. under the first emperor of China, builder of the Great Wall, who made the area known as Kuei-chun. Many groups of people, chiefly Chuang people, must have already been in existence there when the Ch'in and Han Chinese first emerged. A good many northern Chinese then moved southwestward to occupy the more habitable lands near the river and drove the native Chuang people inland and up into the mountainous parts.

As the early northern Chinese never had the European idea of colonization or the American way of creating a reservation area, the native Chuang people were left to live in their own way. But the northern Chinese made life hard for them by extorting high prices for daily commodities such as salt which the Chuang people could not easily come by in the depths of the mountains. The Chinese demanded for one pound of salt thirty or more pounds of rice. Though the Chuang became poorer and poorer and more and more hard-pressed, they managed to live on and maintain their own traditions and customs. The Chuang people are still the largest minority people of China. One most interesting fact I found out was that they had never been much influenced by or accepted Confucian teachings. For instance, in one area called Tou-yang there is a local custom, 碰蛋節 , a p'eng tan chieh, or "egg-hitting festival," held on the third day of the third month of the Chinese lunar calendar. On that day every man and woman, old and young, put on their best clothes and feast with dances and singing all day long. The young men and girls hold red-painted eggs in their hands. Any young man can try to hit the red egg in the hand of his chosen girl. If the girl allows her egg to be hit, it means that she accepts him and they both then dance off to a special place for a talk and to draw up the marriage arrangement. This means that the young people have a free choice of their life partners, whereas under the Confucian tradition the match is arranged by the parents. While I was in Kuei-lin, I asked one of the local people if I might go and join the Tou-yang egg-hitting festival. There was nothing to prevent me, he said, but added the proviso that I might not be able to get my own red egg hit. We laughed.

Ever since the establishment of the new government in Peking in 1949, the Chuang people, as one of the fifty minorities within China, have been given their long-deserved human rights to govern themselves; thus the place formerly called Kwangsi Province is now the Kwangsi Chuang Autonomous Region. The leaders of the Chuang people are in charge of the welfare and care of the Chuang people. I feel more than gratified to know that our Chuang brothers and sisters have gained their living rights in China. This teaches me that the new government not only tries to feed the whole population well, but cares for them individually also. What a satisfaction it is to my personal feelings as a China-born Chinese. From this example, I can also imagine how other minority Chinese nationals are cared for in Sinkiang, Kansu, Tibet, and elsewhere.

Kuei-lin, formerly a city of beautiful scenery for wealthier tourists and artists, has now become a fast-growing industrial center with more than 260 light industrial factories. Most of the workers are the local Chuang people who now have quite a different life from their forefathers. A famous old winery of the city, producing the San-hua-chiu, or "Three-flower wine," has greatly increased its products to meet the growing demand, for this wine is now almost a national drink.

Kuei is the name of a flowering tree peculiar to China; it has the Latin name *Damanthus Fragrans,* but I have never seen it growing anywhere outside China. It is of two kinds, one with tiny yellow flowers and the other with white flowers in clusters at the bases of leaves along the twigs. Both have a strong scent which carries a good distance. As the trees growing around this city are chiefly Kuei trees, so the city gets its name Kuei-lin, or ''Kuei forest.'' Kuei flowers with their strong scent have been manufactured into a special kind of perfume. They have also long been added to cakes and candies, which were great favorites with me in my young days. I tried to buy a few now to revive my memory of the good taste before I caught my plane for Canton.

Inside the plane I composed the following short verse:

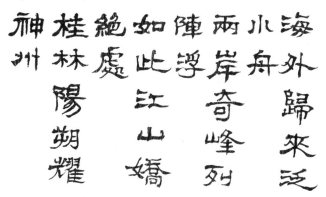

Returning from abroad to travel on a small boat,
Strange peaks standing like soldiers pass on either bank.
River and mountains so marvelously beautiful;
Both Kuei-lin and Yang-shuo glorify our divine land.

My two daughters and their husbands had already come from Nan-ch'ang to greet me at the airport. They wanted to be with me for every possible moment. I knew how much they were attached to me; my forty-two years' absence from them was far too long. Now I had to leave them for my return journey to New York. It was a hard moment for us all, though we realized that nothing could keep me for a moment longer. I noticed my daughters' eyes were wet, but they bravely held back their tears. My feelings were very mixed at the time. While I had to leave them, yet I was happy to have seen how well they had developed into useful womanhood. I was thinking forward to our next meeting as I had promised. I reflected how the new rulers of China had set the country in good order and enabled my youngsters and all their generation and the next to live properly with their deserved human rights.

X I

What It Meant to Me

THIS TRIP of mine to revisit China started on April 15, 1975, and ended on June 15—exactly sixty days. Sixty days are not enough to see even one-fiftieth of the immense land of China, which is bigger than all the fifty States of America combined. Nevertheless, apart from having fulfilled my first aim, to see my kinsfolk after forty-two years, I managed to go round to about twenty centers within eight provinces and to visit a good many communes, factories, and excavation sites. This would have been quite impossible in the old days, for lack of roads, railways, and airplanes. In the descriptions of my travels, I have expressed my reactions from time to time. Here I want to sum up what this trip actually meant to me.

First of all, the feeling of peace and prosperity in the air everywhere was the most striking change from the days when I lived in China, with not one moment free from strife in some area. The old and young I met never mentioned the word *war* all those sixty days. They were all willing to work and help their fellow countrymen.

Another point is China's technical advances. In my university days when I studied chemistry we all realized that one of China's weaknesses was her lack of scientific knowledge. She was known as a very backward country, though all admitted the greatness of her old civilization. I have heard people speak about backward China all the years of my life abroad. Like anybody else, I was most startled when the explosion of China's first atom bomb was announced over the American brodcasting system. I admired wholeheartedly those Chinese scientists who, under the Peking government's guidance, had concentrated their collective effort and determination to achieve this feat, and in complete secrecy. This proved to me that anything could be achieved given enough determination. In the history of our world, any drastic change in a nation's political basis has involved harsh and even cruel actions which alienate the sympathies of the public or cause violent opposition. What I admire about the new government in Peking is that, despite a great upheaval in planning that brought an entirely new policy into being, but without ruthless measures at the same time, it concentrated energy on defense work so thoroughly as to be able to produce the nuclear bomb after only ten years in power.

Third, China has a population of more than eight hundred million now, though it was not so large before. To keep her big population sufficiently fed has been China's greatest problem throughout her long history. The T'ang poet, Tu Fu, who wrote, "Within the red gates wine and meat growing rank;/ On the road are the bones of those frozen to death," was clearly complaining that the rich never cared for the poor. In the China I knew before 1933, Tu Fu's comment was still true. When Japan capitulated in 1945, the extension of civil war in China left the poor in a desperate state. I read the following description of the situation by the famous artist, Chi Pai-shih, then ninety years of age:

> In 1947 and 1948, the people's joy about the Japanese capitulation had long disappeared. The then so-called official currency reached its last stage, almost becoming waste paper to throw about. A small baked bun cost 100,000 dollars and a tiny bread loaf 200,000 dollars. One needed ten million dollars for a meal in a small restaurant. All this was a shock to the world. Later the Chungking Nationalist Government changed the bank-notes into gold-dollar notes. One gold-dollar note equalled three million ordinary dollar-notes. When it was first changed it acted as a little stimulation to the market, but it soon became even worse than the official currency with the price of daily commodities changing minute by minute.

I was then living in Oxford and this description gave me terrible pain in my heart for I could not imagine how my family would manage to survive. The Americans had given one billion dollars in military aid and another billion in economic aid, but those who were running the Nationalist Government cared very little about whether the people had food or not. Everybody was on the verge of starvation, while the high Nationalist officials escaped to Formosa.

It can well be imagined how much it meant to me upon my arrival in China when I saw that now everybody had enough to eat, all eight hundred million of them. The world is said to suffer from the acute shortage of food nowadays, but those eight hundred million Chinese should not be counted among the needy, for the new government in Peking is managing to feed all of them quite adequately.

Mao Tse-tung once wrote, "The people, only the people, are the primeval force to create world history." The fundamental policy of the new government in Peking is set on the welfare of the people of China. The Chinese people are the force to create a new history of China. While in Peking I paid a visit to my old friends, Dr. Wu Yu-shun, deputy president of the Chinese Academy of Sciences, and Dr. Yen Chi-tzu, the noted physicist of the same institute. They took me to lunch in a noted restaurant and while we enjoyed our meal, Dr. Wu told me about 農 *Nung,* 輕 *Ching* 重 *Chung,* Chairman Mao's three-word guideline for the economic policy of the new government. *Nung* represents agriculture; *Ching,* light industry; and *Chung,* heavy industry. The basic aim is the improvement of agriculture in order to produce more food to feed the whole population; the second is to set up light industries, as many as possible; and the third is the building up of heavy industries as well.

An old peasant who is happy to see the result of a good harvest in north China.

In my sixty days of travels I saw many examples of agricultural development, especially at the model production brigade at Tachai where the peasants had changed the barren land into a fertile green one. Further, following Mao Tse-tung's principles to improve agricultural methods and increase production, the people have discovered better methods of irrigation, using the Yellow River, the Yangtze River, and the Huai River. Much work in repairing dykes, building dams, and constructing canals and reservoirs has already been accomplished. Droughts and floods are no longer to be feared.

In my university days I had a good friend, Yang Wei-yi, also of Kiangsi Province, who was an expert in dealing with the locust plagues on rice or other crops and who was sent to destroy masses of horrible locusts in the northern provinces year after year. I had lost touch with him for many years, but on asking commune workers about the locust trouble while I was in the north, they all told me that they had not seen a single locust for years. This is another accomplishment to have got rid of those insects so harmful to the crops.

The new government in Peking has systematically built, according to its policy, more factories for *Ching,* or light industry, in almost every county of every province. Most cities have at least one or two factories manufacturing chemical fertilizers to help agricultural production as well as spinning mills to provide more cloth for local consumption. This may help to explain why everyone in China now has clothes to wear and enough to eat, as they did not before.

With the great development in agriculture and with so many factories functioning, almost everyone is a worker in one way or another. Unemployment is not a question in China now. The so-called modern progressive countries in Europe and both North and South America could not make such a claim. As all the Chinese now have fixed wages, none of them need worry about their next meal, like their forefathers, and they all seem to have spare money to buy what they like. I noticed that most of the city and country market places were full of shoppers in the late afternoon, whenever I happened to be there.

I was impressed by the means whereby the new government in Peking had persuaded the Chinese masses to work so well and effecitvely in the communes and factories. Formerly the bulk of the great Chinese masses could neither read nor write. They were simply forced to work to get something to eat and feed their children, and to pay rent to their landlords and taxes to the government. As they could not read, they were often cheated and fooled by corrupt landlords and officials. The only way to help the people out of the predicament was to educate them. It was well-known before I left China in 1933 that there were only 20 per cent of the four hundred million Chinese who could read and write. When I was in China in April, May, and June of 1975, I was told that 90 per cent or even 95 per cent of the eight hundred million had some education. This must be regarded as a miraculous achievement in only twenty-five years.

With their new-found literacy, all the peasants and workers could attend classes in communes and factories as well as join discussions on socialism and

Learning Mao Tse-tung's writings together.

Mao Tse-tung Thought. Through this study they could understand the government's policy of growing more food and producing more manufactured goods, and this in turn made them want to work harder and combine their efforts. I could now understand why all the peasants I met in the different communes and the workers in various factories all worked so industriously and with a good will. It is little wonder that China now has no unemployment.

An ingenious device has helped to broaden and raise the level of education. During their period of work in communes or factories, young middle school graduates have to join the political study groups as well as help teach those who cannot yet read and write. This has proved to be most effective and rewarding.

Not only does it help to solve the problem of having to build an enormous number of schools and employ many more teachers, but the youngsters can make the workers and peasants, old and young, understand the government's policies as well as contribute their own energy to its materialization. The young graduates who had been with their parents at home since babyhood are glad to have a change of place working in the communes and factories while the local peasants and workers can enjoy having new and young companions to tell them things they did not know before. By such daily exchange of views in conversation,

An old peasant teaching young boys and girls about rice planting.

those who were illiterate before can pick up new knowledge faster and more effectively than they could from school.

Further, the new government in Peking employs a good many artists to create popular and easily understandable pictures in the manner of the old *Yang-liu-ching nien-hua,* 楊柳青年畫 (New Year pictures in colored block printing made at a place called Yang-liu-ching) which have been very popular for country people to buy during the New Year celebration. Though similar in style, the new kind of New Year picture portrays various aspects of the government's policies, such as how the Liberation Army helped the people or how the people are cared for by the government. Apart from these, many large posters with pictures or stories are pasted up at street corners in towns and also in country villages, all of which have the function of teaching people what is going on among them. They educate through mass educational means and get quicker results.

Similarly, the new government in Peking realized that the tunes of the old Peking operas as well as the many folk songs from the various provinces were deeply rooted in the minds of the people, many of whom could at least hum them. So writers were employed to compose new words for the old tunes, indicating government policies, theories of socialism, and Mao Tse-tung's Thought. In addition, they gathered together experienced or newly trained opera and folk singers and set them to perform in different communes and factories. This produced a more penetrating and lasting effect on the ordinary people than any other means.

All the energy and ability of the artists and writers of China today is concentrated on the creation of work that is valuable for the Chinese masses.

Another innovation struck me with particular force when I revisited China: I saw many men and women, old and young, working together in the communes and factories. It showed me that the Chinese woman's position has been raised to

A woman worker shucking corn.

equality with men. This is the greatest turnabout that has happened in China since the second century B.C. Since the western Han period, when Confucianists became the administrators of the government, the difference between men and women had been highly stressed and, in fact, women were set apart on a lower level of society from men. The Confucianists had a saying that it is a virtue for women to be without intelligence, 女子無才便是德 . They stressed that a woman's life has three stages of obedience: At home she obeys her father's will; after marriage she obeys her husband's will; and if her husband dies, she obeys her son's will. In other words, she has no will of her own and cannot live by herself for she has no knowledge of anything and would be unable to work. There had never been any jobs set aside for women to do except embroidering, housework, or serving as wet nurses. Throughout the whole history of China the very few women who were educated could almost be counted on the fingers. Now I saw women working in responsible positions. In fact, many youngish women took the lead in showing me around the communes, factories, and museums. This means that any woman in China now can earn a livelihood with her own ability and be absolutely independent without relying on others to support her.

I remember how in my young days many women I knew, among my relations, for instance, never had the chance or ability to get a job and they had to put up with whatever type of husband they happened to marry. Some men could be quite cruel or, being annoyed with the loss of a job or some other misfortune,

An old peasant woman happy to talk to her family on the telephone for the first time.

could run into a temper and even beat their wives. Those wives had to be submissive and take the beating or whatever it might be, for they could not run away to live by themselves. This attitude explains why very few divorce cases occurred in China in the past.

Apart from those who were born into wealthy families, no woman enjoyed a proper life as a human being. If she was a second or third child in a poor household, she would not receive as much food as her brothers. If famine or drought occurred when she reached the age of ten or more, she would be the one to be sold to a rich family as a maidservant so that her parents could make use of the little payment to keep them alive for a while. The first day she entered the house to which she had been sold, years of misery began. It seldom happened that those who could afford to buy a maid would not try to get their money's worth; they would drive the tender-aged girl to work as hard as she could, though occasionally the girl might find a kindhearted mistress. On top of all her troubles, the old master as well as the young master of the house would take advantage of her youthful face and innocent mind to seduce her. Should that happen and be found out by the mistress, the girl would be severely scolded or even half beaten to death. She could not run back to her parents for help or go to a nearby police station, for she would be sent back immediately. Throughout the past history of China, countless unhappy girls must have died by torture or for some misdeed for which they were not to blame. China in past centuries was always known to the world as being well ruled by great Confucianist scholars. And no Western students of Chinese philosophy would find these miseries for Chinese women in the Confucian classics. I am sure that Confucius did not mean that Chinese women should be treated in such a bad way. It was the later Han Confucianist scholars, who reinterpreted his words, who were to blame.

Those well-known Confucianist scholars in the past would even allow men to have more than one wife and several concubines quite legally, for the purpose of getting a male offspring to continue the family line. Many men took second and third wives with several concubines when they already had one or more sons, simply because they had money to do so and it was quite legal. There were men who could keep their many women together in peace on the surface, but many others would have no peace at home at all. On the other hand, the Confucianists even established laws to discourage women from remarrying if their husbands died before them. In the old days many widows lived most miserable lives until their deaths. Many young betrothed girls even had to go to live in the young man's home as widows if their betrothed died before they married. Many of these girls never married and simply pined away from lack of sympathy.

My most beloved sister married at twenty and already had two sons and a daughter when her husband died. She started her widowhood at twenty-eight. As my mother died when I was only five, before her marriage, my sister looked after me most carefully and lovingly. After her mariage she would come to see me from time to time, to make my clothes and prepare food for me as before. As the general public opinion was so strong then, my sister never gave a thought to remarrying, and no one in the family thought of advising her to do so. After graduating from the university, I left home to take up various jobs and only saw her occasionally. She continued to care for her children as her only interest in life. When I eventually left China for England, my correspondence with her was severed by the Japanese invasion of China. At the end of World War II in 1945, I heard she had moved to live with her young son in the hinterland of Kiangsi Province. I still hoped to see her again one day, but to my regret and pain she died in July 1974 at the age of eighty. The untold sufferings in her life and her long widowhood of fifty years were due to the inhuman precepts of the Confucianist scholars.

Although I was brought up in a traditional Confucian family, I never had any good feeling about this unequal treatment of women, and especially their being forbidden to remarry while men could. While living in Europe and America, I taught Confucianism in my courses. But whenever I heard praises of Confucianism from Western scholars of Chinese, I could not help teasing them about chewing the Chinese Confucian classics word by word without probing into their practical value. So I am very happy to see that the new China has completely erased this bad tradition and that women and men have equal rights in all respects.

Another false distincton that existed in the old China was that between the town dwellers and the countryfolk. In the past as I knew it, these two parts of the population seldom met and mixed together. The countryfolk were always too much occupied with their labor in the fields and did not know what was going on outside their own huts and villages, while the town dwellers had simply no interest in the countryside, found the life there dull, and looked down on the peasants for being illiterate. In this way, though China has never had any castes like the Indians or aristocrats like the English, there were these two different types of people who did not harmonize with one another.

I can give an example from my own relations. I had an uncle on my mother's side, who had managed to accumulate much wealth. In his family he employed many menservants and maids, but he had no son or daughter. Since, according to China's age-old tradition, a man must have a male descendant to carry on the family name to posterity, this uncle had a good reason to take another wife, but each time an arrangement was made, his jealous first wife managed to upset it. Eventually the uncle secretly kept a woman in a house he bought for her some distance from his real home. It was not always easy for him to make excuses to leave home, and after several months the secret was discovered by his wife's spies. The wife, taking several of her close maids and servants with her, dashed to the new house and stabbed the kept woman severely. Some terrible wounds were inflicted and the wounded woman, being from the countryside and not a local city dweller, could not get help from the law. She eventually died from her wounds.

That aunt of mine was not only jealous, but very snobbish and spiteful as well. When I was young—about eleven years old—I was taken to visit this uncle and aunt. The aunt was interviewing some country girls whom she intended to employ as maids. She spoke to three young women with most objectionable remarks: One "had a sour face," the second was "unbearably plain looking," and the third was "oh, such a gluttonous-looking creature." I felt uncomfortable about these remarks and thought she need not say such things, especially if she did not intend to employ the girls. But these differences between the town dweller and the countryfolk were so deeply ingrained, they just could not get on together. I am glad to see now that the differences between these two types of people are fast disappearing.

The movement for many young high school graduates to leave the towns or cities and work in the communes in the countryside is bound to help greatly in leveling the differences between the countryfolk and town dwellers, for as they live together, they will learn from one another. Furthermore this will be most useful in breaking down the barriers of dialect among people from different regions. Unlike India, Africa, and the Arab countries, China has only one language, but many different dialects. Because of the enormous size of the country, with no good roads for communication in the past, people tended to live in one area, without much movement outside it, from one generation to another. By and by their pronunciation of the words twisted and changed. The sound of spoken Chinese thus varied from place to place. The Chinese language is not an alphabetical one, but was originally a set of pictorial images which had to be modified and new ones evolved to meet the requirements from time to time. In the early days of the Chou period, when China was composed of a number of states, the way of writing the pictorial images varied slightly from one state to another, each state designing its own style. Therefore one word or character had several forms. Fortunately the first emperor of Ch'in, who reigned from 221 to 207 B.C., built the Great Wall, abolished the Chou feudal system, and united all states into one empire, decided to use the form of writing of the Ch'in state as the official and only form. Thus the country was unified by using only one form of writing for the common language. It became the instrument for perpetuating Chinese civilization from the Ch'in days to the present. It has helped to unite many different races within China.

Differences in the pronunciation of the official language still remain because of the enormous area with little means for communication. Different dialects exist in the various areas, but all are represented by the same written form. It has long been a practice for two Chinese from two remote areas who could not understand each other's speech to communicate by writing. However, conversation through writing has obvious drawbacks. So the elimination of the different dialects and the establishment of one standard form of speech—*P'u-t'ung-hua,* 普通話, "common language"—is the ideal goal. Most young high school graduates are able to speak this common language and can easily influence their co-workers in the communes and factories. Though we all understand that it is not easy to eliminate the age-old dialects in a short time, I was most happy to have seen the first movement in this direction and the good results that the new government in Peking has achieved in the dialect-elimination movement within only twenty-five years. Of course modern broadcasting in the common language to every area is very helpful too. I at least found no difficulty in making myself understood in many different places in my travels.

Another great development in China is the universal medicare which has extended to all Chinese, both countryfolk and town dwellers. In the old China that I

An old expert on foot troubles.

remember, any country people who became ill, even seriously ill, would not be able to find doctors at all in many places, for no doctor cared to make a living in the countryside. The well-trained old-fashioned Chinese doctors tended to live in big cities and the country peasants could not afford to visit them. Some knowledge of the general function of various herbs had been handed down by word of mouth from one generation to the next for centuries and helped many of those living in the remote inland areas, when they were ill, and had no doctor to advise them.

After China became a Republic in 1911, a number of sizable hospitals where poor people could go for treatment were established by Christian missionary bodies, with some assistance from the local government in many of the larger towns. However, this only benefited those who were living within easy reach. Those in the countryside, far away, were quite helpless; when seriously ill they simply waited and hoped to get better. Often they died without any medical attention. The Nationalist government did nothing to solve the old problem. Now it is very different; each commune and factory has one resident doctor, at least,

A teacher demonstrating the application of an acupuncture needle.

and some nurses. It surprised me to see the masses in China able to enjoy medicare as do their counterparts in the Western world. Besides, the ancient Chinese technique of acupuncture has become known and widespread in Europe and North America in the last ten years. It has been studied scientifically and given considerable approval in general practice. China can say for certain that there is practically no venereal disease there anywhere.

Lastly, I must record my pleasure in the unusual flowering of archaeology that has been blooming so wonderfully in China since 1950. I say "unusual," for the term *archaeology* was little known in China before the 1920s, though some ancient relics had come to light from time to time since early days, even in the first or second centuries B.C. In my younger days, my father often expressed his cherished wish to go to Peking to see the only museum in the country, the Palace Museum which contained many well-known masterpieces. But father's wish had never been realized. There were no small art galleries or museums anywhere else. Now to my great joy I found many museums with more art objects, newly excavated, than there was room to display them in almost every place I visited. There was even a tiny museum on Lu Mountain. It meant a lot to me.

In 1954 I happened to buy a new publication entitled *Chung-kuo chi-pen chien-chu kung-cheng chu-tou wen-wu chan-lan tu-l'u* (Catalogue of art objects unearthed during early building operation throughout the country). It had a long introduction by the late Cheng Cheng-to, a great writer on art and literature who met an untimely death in a flying accident. Cheng described how, since the establishment of the new government in 1949, with the many new constructions of factories, reservoirs, dams, railroads, and public roads, a huge number of art objects had come to light. Within only four years, about a hundred forty thousand pieces had been excavated. In the catalogue about thirty-seven hundred pieces were selected for exhibition. As these discoveries were totally unexpected, a good number of them were unintentionally broken or destroyed by the construction workers who had had no knowledge of such things before. But they soon learned to be careful in their digging and they knew they should report immediately to their headquarters if they came across anything unusual; then experts and archaeologists would be summoned to examine them. Since that exhibition in 1954 all construction workers have been warned to look out for buried treasures and many systematic excavations have been carried out too. The Chinese Academy of Sciences established a special section for archaeological study and has published two specialized magazines, 文 物, *Wen-wu,* or "Art objects," and 考 古, *Kao-ku,* or "Archaeology," every month since 1971. From these magazines, which I have been receiving regularly for the past five years, I have learned more about China's past than I ever knew before. And the workers themselves, in building factories, dams, or railroads, began to learn much about China's past too. Sound evidence about the early periods of China's history is being discovered from the new excavations.

For the past two or three centuries, if not more, the Chinese have been known to the Western world as ardent worshippers of their ancestors. The digging up of any other family's tomb used to be regarded as the greatest crime. This is one of the reasons why little archaeological study had been done before. Who would have imagined that all the building work, including the housing projects for the people, would have produced from the earth so many great art treasures of China's past? There followed a serious study of the ancient royal tombs and the tombs of noblemen and other great families. It was the ancient tradition in China, as in Egypt, that when an important personage, say, an emperor or empress, a prince or princess, died, the treasures that he cared most about in his life would be buried with him in his tomb. For centuries China was familiar with tomb burglary and most of the famous art objects which have been exhibited in Western museums were stolen originally from tombs in China and were sold through middlemen—the art dealers. But the present finds from the recently excavated tombs have been designated national treasures and may not be removed from the country. Many of them have never been known before, such as the two enormous square *Tings* of the Shang period, which I saw in the Chengchow Museum.

Formerly only two ancient Shang sites were known, now there are eight of them, each of which contains many art objects of the period. The Pan P'o site excavated in 1964 contains the earliest house foundation, six thousand years old; hundreds of Neolithic painted potteries were unearthed there too. I also saw the excavation still being carried on at Ta-ho-ts'un in Honan Province as well as the tombs of the Ming emperor Wan Li in Peking; of Princess Yung-tai; and that of Prince Chang-huai in Sian, Shensi Province; and many others.

Perhaps the most startling recent find was the discovery, in the latter part of 1974, of a large ditch in fromt of the tomb of the first emperor of Ch'in, Shih-huang-ti, in Lin-t'ung in which were six thousand life-sized figures and horses

A drawing from the T'ang fresco in Prince Chang-huai's tomb, from about the eighth century.

made of pottery from the third century B.C. This find of life-sized figures not only provides interesting evidence about early Chinese armor, uniforms, headdresses, and hair styles from those ancient days, but also alters the old conception that China never produced large sculptured works like those in Egypt and Greece.

When the exhibition of Archaeological Finds of the People's Republic of China was held in Europe and America recently, one particular object—the pottery figure of a seated woman, unearthed in 1964 at Lin-t'ung, Shensi, and dated 221–207 B.C.—raised many doubts among Western scholars. They could not believe it was such an early work, for no similar type of human figure had ever appeared in China before. The recent find of six thousand life-sized soldiers and horses from the same area dispelled such doubts completely.

Archaeologists everywhere are now changing their views after so many new discoveries; some aspects of China's history will have to be rewritten. With all these new materials coming out of the earth, our knowledge of Chinese art in the past has been enormously enriched. Those specially interested in it are encouraged to make careful study. After this trip of mine to revisit China in 1975 I was greatly inspired by the hope of one day writing a new book on the history of Chinese art with additional illustrations of the newly excavated relics. My sole aim is to let the world know more about Chinese art, one of the chief flowers of Chinese civilization, and to help others in other parts of the world to have a fuller and more thorough understanding of it.

Epilogue

THOUGH I TRAVELED to a good many places and saw a great many things within the sixty days of my stay, it was really only a fraction of the immense China, with her three thousand years of history. Yet the little I saw convinced me of the great change that had taken place during the forty-two years of my absence. One cannot hope for a complete picture in a limited time and I have to be content with what I gained for the time being.

On my return to New York, not only did many of my American friends want to hear about what I had found in present-day China, but friends in Europe, particularly in England, and also in Australia wanted to learn of my experience—hence the writing of this book. I hope my readers will realize that I could not possibly visit so many places and see as much in only two months as in the years when I

A road worker.

lived in China. On the other hand, I enjoyed the obvious advantages of modern travel, with the many new roads, railways, and airports through which China is advancing into the modern world. The great development of air travel directly after World War II has shortened distances immeasurably. I could never forget my thirty-three-day sea voyage from Shanghai to England in June 1933. I can now fly to Peking from New York in less than two days.

To answer my friends' questions about my impressions of China now and my predictions for her future from this visit is too tall an order. The questions are too wide-ranging and no one could answer them in a few words. Besides, China is a country of eight hundred million people and how could I, a mere one, speak for so many? However, one thing is absolutely certain, this great mass of eight hundred million has become unified and mutually supportive, more than ever before in their history. In the past the Chinese people earned the reputation of being like 盤散沙, or *yi-p'an san-sha*, "a dish of separated grains of sand," no two attached to one another. Most people in the world have heard about the great Confucian traditions in China, but few realize that Confucian principles only linked together the family members but not society outside the family. Even the great Taoist teachings center on personal goodness and the cultivation of the individual spirit, without much thought for others. China had been governed for centuries by Confucian scholars; it is a deplorable fact that so many Confucian scholars, in one period after another, never attempted to educate the bulk of the masses but preferred to keep them in the dark. As long as China remained isolated, as she was for hundreds of years, that kind of blind administration by the so-called Confucian scholars' politics could be perpetuated, but as soon as China was attacked and penetrated by outside forces, she found herself lost. Her great helpless masses could do nothing to save her.

The most striking thing, perhaps, that I found during my sixty-day stay was that the new China had concentrated her main efforts on educating the masses.

An old college teacher discussing vegetables with his students.

Individuals have been made to realize that they belong to the whole country and all have their part to play, their contribution to make, and their obligation to defend their country when it is in danger. To provide even a minimum of education for eight hundred million is not an easy task, nor can it be done within a short number of years. Yet the new China achieved it in the past twenty-six years—little short of a miracle.

As I mentioned in the beginning of this book, for a century past China had been defeated again and again without the people having any understanding of what was happening to them. Nowadays, their knowledge and political consciousness have been raised to such a point that they could not easily be influenced or controlled by a small section of the population any more. And China could not be destroyed by any outside force in the future. This is something I am quite sure of.

In her long past China was ruled by one person's pleasure, whether a monarch or a dictator such as the short-lived Yüan Shih-kai or the so-called Generalissimo Chiang Kai-shek. Any appointment of subordinates was entirely in their hands, and the ability of the men of their choice was not always the main consideration. This could only lead to failure and disaster in the end. But the new China, as I see her, has a constitution clearly laid down and is ruled by a party and a State Council with the collective aim of doing good for the country. That is why I am convinced that China's future is good and bright.

I am neither a propagandist, nor an ideologist; I simply want to live by good principles and to do good for others as a human being should. I have tried to describe objectively what I saw in China past, before 1933, and what I experienced in present-day China. My readers should be able to draw their own comparisons between these two periods and to see the differences. I need not add any comment about whether the change that took place was good for the people or not: It should be self-evident. China is a very old country and needed a great change badly. But these great changes could not evolve of their own accord; they needed some great, faithful, and devoted men to bring them about. I cannot help expressing my admiration for the three devoted leaders who have just died: Mao Tse-tung, Chu Teh, and Chou En-lai, as well as for their faithful followers.

I was only a few years younger than those three—Mao, Chu, and Chou—and have watched closely their sixty-year devotion to working for the great changes in China, undauntedly and without respite. Each of them escaped death by a hairbreadth many a time. In fact, during my terms of office as civil governor in three different counties, I received telegraph messages twenty-seven times from the Nanking government's headquarters that Marshal Chu Teh and Chairman Mao Tse-tung had been killed in the fighting. I feel gratified that each of the three great heroes died a natural death and that they had actually seen their work come to fruition during their lifetimes. They must have felt happy that they had trained many faithful followers to carry on their work, and to know that their eight hundred million fellow countrymen, having enough to eat and plenty of work to do, would always remember what they had done for them, though none of the three expected anything in return from their people. I cannot sufficiently express my admiration for them, so devoted in their work and so utterly selfless; and none of the three left any descendants endowed with unnecessary power and wealth. One thing is certain, without their lifelong efforts, the great changes could never have been achieved and China's misery would not have ended.

China's civilization has remained unbroken from the beginning of her history till the present day. Unlike those of other ancient civilizations, such as the Egyptians, the Greeks, and the Indians, none of whose early languages are still in use, the Chinese written language has never undergone a big change in form. Besides, the Chinese have never been divided into different religions or castes, nor have they any hereditary aristocracy. In the past dynasties, members of the imperial families as well as higher officials were ennobled, but their rank was not inherited or passed down to their descendants. Again, a Chinese Confucian scholar was neither a theologian nor a priest and, though the Confucian tradition was centuries old, it never held people together as a religious faith was able to do with its services in churches or mosques. This may be the reason why China was able to uproot her age-old traditions and transform herself into a completely new socialist state within only twenty-five years. The large bulk of the Chinese people, when educated, could stand on equal footing with those so-called educated Confucian scholars, without any religious or caste differences. No other country could easily achieve this.

To my way of thinking, China's complete change from the past is a sure sign not only that she is revitalizing herself, but also that she will infuse new life into the other nations of the world. Human history has lasted a hundred centuries, if not more, and the world has grown old, too old, with endless stories of bloody killings: one by one at first, then group by group, and eventually nation by nation, with the future possibility that millions may be killed by nuclear bombing. I dread to think of nuclear warfare in the future. Some fundamental change has to be found and worked out. Social ills have been accumulating far too much now and they will have to be wiped out altogether, not by religious sermons or by moral conscience. Perhaps what China has achieved in the past twenty-five-odd years could be taken as the first step to revitalize mankind. I need to see more of China and to give more proof of these hopeful thoughts and predictions as long as I have life and strength.